confessions of a
raging perfectionist

AMANDA JENKINS

TYNDALE HOUSE PUBLISHERS, INC.
CAROL STREAM, ILLINOIS

Visit Tyndale online at www.tyndale.com.

TYNDALE and Tyndale's quill logo are registered trademarks of Tyndale House Publishers, Inc.

Designed by Jennifer Ghionzoli

Edited by Stephanie Rische

Published in association with the literary agency of WordServe Literary Group, Highlands Ranch, CO, www.wordserveliterary.com.

ISBN 978-1-4143-7870-1

Printed in the United States of America

19	18	17	16	15	14	13
7	6	5	4	3	2	1

FOR DALLAS, *who loves me in spite of my flaws.*
AND FOR MY MOM, *who doesn't know I have them.*

contents

Acknowledgments *ix*

Introduction *xi*

acknowledgments

TO MY MOM AND DISCUSSION-QUESTIONS COWRITER:
Growing up, I watched you be a student of the Word, poring over it and praying on a regular basis. I also watched you be brave enough to tell the truth about the things you were struggling with. You taught me to be authentic and to take my junk to the Lord. This book wouldn't exist without your example. Thank you for your constant cheerleading and for taking some of the work off my shoulders.

TO MY AMAZING HUSBAND:
You've somehow managed to be both a truth teller and a soft place to fall, and to love me all the time. My messy heart is safe with you, and that's a gift I don't take for granted.

TO MY DEAR FAMILY AND TREASURED IN-LAWS:
Y'all have walked alongside me in my good moments and in my yucky moments. Thank you for your truly unconditional love and grace, and for always pointing me back to Jesus.

TO MY FRIENDS WHO WERE WILLING TO LEND ME YOUR STORIES:
Thank you for being a part of this project and a part of my journey. Life really is a tapestry, and your stories have changed me and drawn me closer to the Lord.

TO MY HARVEST FAMILY:

Dallas and I are so blessed to attend a church where Christ is highly exalted and everything else is put into perspective. Love doing life together.

AND TO TYNDALE HOUSE PUBLISHERS:

Thank you for taking a chance on me and for being patient with my perfectionism throughout the entire process (since I'm clearly not in full remission . . . yet).

introduction

THIS IS NOT A BOOK. Well, *now* it's a book, but it didn't start out that way. It began as my journal—a way to keep track of all the yucky things God was showing me about myself and what I've come to know as my addiction to perfection.

And I *am* addicted. Like most perfectionists, I want everything in my life to be beautiful. I want my home to look fabulous, my car to sparkle, and my love handles to disappear. I want my closets to be organized, my children to be well behaved and happy (usually in that order), and my editor to find zero mistakes. I want people to think I have everything under control, and I want to actually have everything under control.

Safe to say, I have a number of unattainable goals. And what's worse—I constantly keep track of how I'm doing to reach those goals. Or not.

Maybe that's why I love the movie *Bridget Jones's Diary*. The plotline centers on Bridget's diary and the drama in her life that becomes its content. She begins each day's entry by listing her stats—pounds gained or lost, cigarettes smoked, men interested, books read, party invites received. She is, to put it mildly, a work in progress—someone who can't get life quite right, no matter

xii III CONFESSIONS OF A RAGING PERFECTIONIST

how hard she tries. And every success and failure is documented in her diary.

Aside from her British accent and chain-smoking, I'm a lot like Bridget Jones. I begin each day with a list—*keep the house picked up, limit myself to one Diet Coke, spend special time with each of my kids, work out, pray, avoid sugar, read a chapter in a book about something important*, and so on and so forth. And then I determine each day's worth by how many of those things I actually did. Like Bridget, pounds gained or lost, items checked off, stuff accomplished.

And I must say, my lists are good. The things I want to do lead to good health and better relationships. While not everything is necessary, a number of things on the list are. After all, bills have to be paid, clothes have to be cleaned, and kids need attention. So, generally speaking, my problem is not my list.

My problem, I've recently realized, is the significance I attach to the list—that if I lose five pounds and spend twenty minutes reading my Bible, I'll be a better, more spiritual, more loving, more *lovable* person. When I fail to live up to my own expectations, I feel inadequate. Or more specifically (and as my stats frequently read), overweight, lazy, disorganized, and unworthy of the approval I seek.

Thing is, I don't think I'm alone. And I don't think perfectionists are the only ones whose identities are wrapped up in impossible goals. Most of the women I know, from our high school babysitter to my precious grandma, base much of their self-worth on stuff that can be crossed off a list. For Christian women, that's a tragic irony—tragic because, like everyone else, we spend most of our time working toward unattainable goals; ironic because Christ died to free us from the notion that we must earn our worth.

So it begs the question: Why do we keep track of our stats? And if we experience time after time the frustration and failure our personal expectations bring, why is it so hard to leave them behind? Is it possible to ever really be free?

Hard to imagine because, as I said, I'm a raging perfectionist, though this book isn't about perfectionism, per se. Instead, it's about how the pursuit of perfection has led me down a very wrong road—one that has produced and nurtured a dozen chapters' worth of strangleholds.

Because the things I've tried to make perfect have become my idols.

In the past few years, God has been working to change my heart and move me toward the only perfect we'll know in this life: Himself. And while that may sound pretty, I assure you it's been rough. Coming to terms with my addiction to perfection has been hard and sad and exhausting—and at times, embarrassing (case in point, this book). But I'm on board with what God is doing; I want freedom.

And so, in an effort to embrace my imperfect reality, every chapter of this book begins with my real stats. I'm hoping my transparency will pry me from the things that have become my idols, loosening their grip on my heart and mind.

And I pray God will use my journey to further yours.

CHAPTER I ⸺ Vanity

Weight: 142 pounds

Calories: 2,260

Pants that are too tight: 3

Wrinkles: 8 too many

Resolve to lose 7 pounds and double up on eye cream.

BEAUTY QUEEN

Tara McClary's a good-lookin' woman—the quintessential Southern belle. Perfectly mannered and manicured, blonde hair and brown eyes, tall, thin, and tan. It's little surprise, then, that in 1990 she and her mom were crowned Mother/Daughter USA. She's a pageant success story, and in truth she's the kind of woman most of us love to hate. Problem is that once you get to know her, you'll have a hard time finding just cause.

I met Tara when I was a junior in college. My boyfriend, Dallas (now my husband), and his family had known the McClarys for years. And after reconnecting in their early twenties, Tara and Dallas came up with an idea for a book they wanted to cowrite. As a non-title-holding, average girl, I felt a bit unsettled when my boyfriend told me he was going to be working for hours on end with a beauty

1

queen. When I expressed my concern, he explained that he didn't think of her that way. She was a family friend, and besides, she wasn't his type; she was too perfect. He preferred the girl next door.

Hmm.

Much to Dal's surprise, I didn't feel better. That is, until I met her. Turns out she wasn't a threat—and not because she wasn't perfect; she kind of was. But she was beautiful without pretense. She was genuinely likable.

The three of us spent the weekend at Dal's parents' house (she to flesh out ideas for the book and me to stand guard), and we got to talking about pageant life. It seemed like a lot of pressure to me—so many beautiful women all competing for the same crown, their bodies and clothing being scrutinized by the judges and, no doubt, by each other. She laughed and agreed. She *had* felt the pressure. But after years of chasing perfection, she realized there would always be someone more beautiful. It made no difference how often she exercised or the number of beauty products she used—someone would always upstage her. So she abandoned the goal of attaining perfection and accepted her limitations and, in turn, herself.

It was simple enough. If Tara McClary had to come to terms with the fact that there would always be someone prettier, even with her beauty credentials, then it was certainly true for me, too. And it sounded great—embracing the idea would be like throwing insecurity to the wind. I'm me, and you're you. If you're prettier, good for you.

Poof. Pressure's off.

Because that's what we do, isn't it? We compare. She's skinnier, she's got bigger boobs, she has perfect hair—and there's no end to the madness. Whether it's a girl in line at the grocery store or celebrities in magazines, we find fault with ourselves based on a standard set by someone else. And dropping out of the race made sense to me.

Problem is that in spite of Tara's wisdom and the freedom it brought her, I haven't been able to stop comparing. Logically speaking, I know I'm running a race I can't win; someone will always out-pretty me. But even when I'm not comparing myself to someone else, I keep an ever-growing list of things I'd like to change. If only I could tighten up my abs and get rid of a few wrinkles, then I'd be content.

Yeah, right.

So if logic doesn't snap me out of my vain haze, how will I be able to accept myself, flaws and all? And since the pressure to be beautiful seems to come from both the inside and the outside, is it even possible to escape it? What's the trick to being happy just to be me?

DOWNHILL FROM HERE

A few weeks ago I had an appointment with a new dermatologist regarding a mole. Since I was already there, I thought I'd ask if something could be done to tame the wrinkles around my eyes. But when I stepped into the lobby, I knew I was in trouble. Turned out the dermatologist's office doubled as a spa, which in LA is code for all things cosmetic—from chemical peels to lip injections. I had a hunch a really good moisturizer wouldn't be the doctor's only recommendation.

And it wasn't. She told me I *did* have a lot of wrinkles, especially for someone so young, but not to worry—with a little Botox she could make me look eighteen again. Um, looking like a teenager hadn't been my initial goal. But somewhere between having my "before" pictures snapped without warning under the fluorescent lights and hearing what my face will look like in ten years without "intervention," eighteen started to sound pretty good.

Truth is, we don't have the money for Botox. Dallas and I have three kids under ten, which means cosmetic intervention doesn't exactly make the short list of things we can afford. And that's a good thing, because it's not just my face that's beginning to fail me. Since I had kids, the whole system seems to be breaking down. Varicose veins have shown up on my thighs, and my armpits sweat for no good reason—sometimes one without the other. I have stretch marks, some explained by pregnancy and others not, and yesterday I realized I'd buttoned some skin into my jeans and it didn't even hurt. Oh—and when I laugh too hard, a little pee comes out.

Varicose veins have shown up on my thighs; my armpits sweat for no good reason, sometimes one without the other. And when I laugh too hard, a little pee comes out.

Yeah, if money weren't an issue, I imagine a lot of procedures would be tempting, which is why we see it time and again in the lives of the rich and famous—first a lift, then a tuck, then an injection of some sort. Watching it play out in Hollywood is enough to prove the whole pursuit is futile or, at best, unending. There are websites devoted to outing celebrities for their surgeries. My favorite sites post the before and after pictures, which have to be updated every time they go under the knife, be it to fix what they had done and don't like or to tweak what they liked but now droops or to tackle a newly aging feature.

And yet we wonder what it would be like to fix that one thing. Ha.

And it's not just cosmetic surgery—it's all the things we do to get pretty and stay pretty. After my third child was born, I was ready to buckle down and get back in shape. For a year and a half I exercised almost every day, watched my diet, and got more rest. I looked really great, too. The baby weight came off, and my friends praised me for being so disciplined. But eventually I got tired of the strict routine. I decided to take a short break, which turned into the past year and a half of infrequent exercise and a lot more sugar.

That's the problem. I don't just feel the pressure to look better, because even when I reach my goal, I have to somehow stay there. I have to maintain. And since maintaining in my thirties is a lot harder than it was in my twenties, it's clear each decade will bring a host of new problems. The pressure never lets up, and once again the race I find myself running is a no-win. I fixate on a flaw, compare myself to someone else, work hard to change, fail to reach my goal, fixate, compare, work hard, reach my goal, fail to maintain.

Sigh.

I'm a mouse on a wheel.

And in my exhaustion, I turn to God. Perhaps He should have been my starting place, but alas . . . I often think of Him as a last resort instead of my first line of defense.

WHEN BEAUTY FLEES

Embarrassed as I am to admit this, a few days ago I was folding laundry while watching TMZ. For some reason, the reporters (I use that term loosely) were showing clips of Janice Dickinson shopping on Melrose Avenue, and I became mesmerized by both her charisma and her ever-changing face. And a verse I'd read sometime before came to mind:

> *People are like grass;*
> *their beauty is like a flower in the field.*
> *The grass withers and the flower fades.*
> *But the word of the Lord remains forever.*
> I PETER 1:24-25, NLT

Janice's life seems to illustrate that verse. She rose to super-model status in the late seventies and was gorgeous to say the least—a huge success. But her career fizzled in the late eighties as she battled addiction and substance abuse. Fast-forward to 2003, when she reemerged as a judge on the reality show *America's Next Top Model*. Four seasons later she left to start her own show, *The Janice Dickinson Modeling Agency*, where she began to build and groom a stable of models she now represents.

It's a great story. A once-famous, now forgotten woman over-comes the odds, gets sober, reinvents herself, and barrels back onto the scene, becoming fabulous and famous once again. But there's a catch. If you look at Janice today, she only resembles the supermodel she once was. Never mind the inevitable aging of the past few decades; to date, she's had at least ten operations, which have left her looking more plastic than real. Ironically, and in spite of her extreme effort to stay beautiful, the clos-est she'll come to her former glory will be to *represent* younger, more beautiful models. Like the rest of us, she'll flourish for a time and then wither. Someone new will bloom, and she'll be forgotten.

It's simply the way of things.

Charm is deceptive, and beauty is fleeting.
PROVERBS 31:30

Beauty doesn't drift quietly into the night. It flees.

*Your life is like the morning fog—it's here a little while,
then it's gone.* JAMES 4:14, NLT

The only people remembered after they die are A-list celebrities and presidents—usually in that order. As for the rest of us? Not so much. Our lives are brief, and we'll be forgotten, no matter how pretty we were. On the other hand, there's a way to be beautiful that our appearance-crazed culture cares far less about.

The LORD does not look at the things people look at. People look at the outward appearance, but the LORD looks at the heart. I SAMUEL 16:7

When I was twenty years old, I was a counselor at a camp for inner-city kids. My first week I was assigned to a group of kindergarten girls who were all adorable—except for Mervina. She was tall and lanky and looked dirty most of the time. Her clothes didn't fit, and her shoes had holes. She put a brown Vaseline-type substance in her hair every day that smelled terrible—probably because it was so old. And she wanted to be near me constantly, holding my hand or sitting in my lap.

Much to my surprise and shame, Mervina wasn't easy for me to love. Her disadvantages should have roused my compassion, but the other girls were so much cuter, and I was shallower than I knew. Thankfully, the Holy Spirit brought the thunder that week and convicted me constantly, which resulted in Mervina getting most of my attention and affection. And the conviction didn't stop there, because God has used that precious little girl to expose the stranglehold beauty has on my heart. Year by year since, He's been helping me see people, including myself, the way *He* does—because God doesn't care what we look like; He sees inside.

It's because of His mercy that God tells us the truth. How sad it must be for Him to see us clinging to false hope and worshiping at the altar of *pretty*. He wants us to abandon the goals of youth and beauty because they promise to disappoint. To whatever degree we have them, we'll lose them, in spite of our best efforts to the contrary.

There's a different way to live. As a loving father, God calls us to lay down our pursuits, along with all the disappointment and burden they bring, and rest.

DIFFERENT KIND OF EYES

Janice Dickinson's desire to be beautiful is not unique, though most of us don't have half her excuse. In her autobiography, Janice writes about her tragic childhood—how she was molested, beaten, and emotionally abused by her father. Every day, in some form or another, he told her she was worthless. I can only assume she believed him.

No doubt Janice has gone to extreme measures to hold on to beauty, but understandably so. I can't begin to know the pressure of having to prove to her wretched father and to herself that she had value. Her beauty gave her that sense of value and earned her a significant place in the world. So yeah, she's extreme. But like her, my worth is tangled up in the way I look and, more specifically, in the way other people see me. Janice is just a louder version of the rest of us.

While we're busy searching for our value, God has already ascribed it.

And it's not the way God intended for us to be. While we're busy searching for value, He's already ascribed it.

We are God's masterpiece. He has created us anew in Christ Jesus, so we can do the good things he planned for us long ago.
EPHESIANS 2:10, NLT

When I look at the world around me, God's artistry is obvious. And as I learned in Sunday school, the same hands that created mountains and sunsets and puppies and the brilliant colors of autumn made each person—including me—with care and purpose. When I fixate on the world's definition of beauty, not only do I inevitably feel bad about myself, but I also miss out on what God has in mind for me—the good things He wants me to do—which ironically always result in making me more beautiful on the inside. God says I'm His masterpiece, which is something I have to sit with for a minute—it's huge. I mean, the same incredible, intentional detail I see in a single flower is evidence that God was specific and intentional in creating me. In His image, no less. I imagine that believing I'm a masterpiece is the first step toward being okay with my aging, imperfect self.

I pray that you, being rooted and established in love,
may have power, together with all the Lord's holy people,
to grasp how wide and long and high and deep is the love
of Christ, and to know this love that surpasses knowledge—
that you may be filled to the measure of all the fullness
of God. EPHESIANS 3:17-19

It's not enough to know we're loved. God wants us to be rooted and established in His love—to be anchored and defined by it, and to see the world through its lens. Wrapping our minds around God's enormous, indescribable, beautiful love for us in Jesus is the key to being happy with the way we've been made.

Unfortunately, I often have a hard time getting those verses from my head to my heart. I have moments of awe when I'm content with God's acceptance, but they don't last long, and sooner or later I'm back to being discouraged by the mirror. Because the immediate gratification beauty offers is powerful; the approval of others is powerful. Recently I've begun to pray that God's love would become more important to me than my desire for outward beauty, more important than my longing to be accepted and admired by others. I'm praying that God would change what matters to me.

How beautiful on the mountains
   are the feet of those who bring good news,
who proclaim peace,

> *who bring good tidings,*
> *who proclaim salvation,*
> *who say to Zion,*
> *"Your God reigns!"*

ISAIAH 52:7

"How beautiful the feet"—love that. I wonder how different my life would be if the beauty of my *feet* were the priority of my life. If my extreme focus on my wrinkles and my dress size died a quick death and my eyes instead became fixed on others and the Good News I so often forget to share. If my gospel-carrying feet got more action than my workout video. If I heeded the call to talk more about salvation in Jesus than about losing five pounds. If I put other people's needs above my desire to be affirmed.

I want beautiful feet.

We can be different. We can be freed from insecurity. We can be content with what we have, and we can develop an inward beauty that stands the test of time. And because the pressure from our beauty-obsessed culture isn't going to let up, we can learn exactly what we'll need to fight back.

SWIMMING UPSTREAM

> *She is clothed with strength and dignity;*
> *she can laugh at the days to come.*

PROVERBS 31:25

I love this verse because I love this woman. She laughs. She's happy and carefree. Bring on the gray hair and belly rolls—nothing can steal her confidence. And I want to be just like her. I would love to laugh at the days to come, because laughing would mean I'm not afraid of them, that my heart is full of joy and my self-worth on solid ground.

So what does this woman have that I don't have? Strength and dignity. It takes strength to push back against the pressures of our culture and to resist the urge to cling to youth. It takes dignity to stand tall in spite of humbling changes in our aging bodies, to reject the notion that we're more valuable if we're beautiful. Strength and dignity have the power to keep us grounded

While vanity is a fierce opponent, strength and dignity are its kryptonite.

in the reality of God's loving acceptance. With them, we can wage war against the constantly critical inner voice and experience a confidence that doesn't ebb and flow. Because while vanity is a fierce opponent, strength and dignity are its kryptonite.

It's time to get back to Sunday school basics: God made us and He loves us. If we believe that, we'll begin to be content with the unique way we've been created. And although the temptation to find our worth in beauty remains, God will provide strength and dignity for the journey.

And we'll laugh.

REAL LIFE

I recently got back in touch with our friend Tara, the beauty queen. She's married now, with seven-year-old twins, Daniel and Caroline. I was sad to find out that for the past year and a half, little Daniel has been fighting leukemia. Their lives have been consumed with doctor visits and chemo. As a mom, I can't imagine how terrifying it must be.

Yet as Tara tells it, God has been her rock, her refuge, and her friend. In journal entries she posts online, Tara talks about the good God has done and continues to do in her life. She has tremendous faith.

Recalling her wisdom twelve years ago, I can't help but wonder

When we misplace our worth and allow our hearts to chase after things that fail, we miss out on a deeper, more meaningful, all-consuming relationship with our loving Creator.

if God got the vanity idol out of Tara's way early on in life to make room in her heart for more of Himself—to help prepare her, in part, for the road ahead. Because when we misplace our worth and allow our hearts to chase after things that fail, we miss out on a deeper, more meaningful, all-consuming relationship with our loving Creator. Tara knows God in that way, and because she does, she rests in Him now.

EXCERPT FROM JOURNAL ENTRY POST #168 ıııııııııııııııııı

Too often, I've been afraid to let others see the real me, and I've camouflaged myself in beauty and poise—but while man sees the cover, God knows my core. And cancer has its own unique way of stripping away my veneer and false pretense. God's process of making us more precious is to take us through fiery trials—not to burn us, but to strip away the self-centeredness that mars the radiance of His reflection in us.

As voiced by Casting Crowns in the song "Stained Glass Masquerade," when I'm full of myself and begin trading the altar in for a stage, I miss out on the tremendous blessings God has designed for my life. Less of me plus more of Him equates to real joy, peace, and fulfillment.

TARA MCCLARY REEVES

CHAPTER 2 ⦚⦚⦚⦚⦚ Money

SEPTEMBER 4

Bills outstanding: 2

Checking account: $2,288 for the month

Savings account: $663

Resolve to avoid Target until payday.

SHOW ME THE MONEY

Jerry Jenkins is a multimillionaire. Out of the 180 books he's published, twenty have reached the *New York Times* Best Sellers List—seven of which debuted at number one. In 2001, his latest release from the Left Behind series was the bestselling novel in the world. He has written biographies for guys like Walter Payton, Nolan Ryan, and Orel Hershiser. He assisted Billy Graham with his memoirs. Safe to say he's had some success as a writer.

He's also my father-in-law.

Truth be told (and the obvious be stated), sharing in the spoils of a parent's flourishing career is nice—we have things and get to experience things we otherwise wouldn't. But there's another side too, because I grew up on the other side of the so-called tracks. So while I enjoy the perks, I struggle with guilt (or pride, I suppose) that I didn't earn the money myself. When it seems like everything Jerry touches turns to gold, I turn a little green—it would be nice to have so much at my disposal, to enjoy the ginormous fruit of our labor. I'm happy my husband's parents have thrived and experienced the good life, because I love them and they're wonderful, generous people, but I'm also sad because my own parents have walked a very different road.

But let's back up.

Jerry's story is pretty great, actually. Sort of rags to riches. He was raised in a lower-middle-class family; his dad was a policeman and his mom was a homemaker. They had four boys, one car, and hand-me-down clothes. Jerry started his career as a sportswriter in the late sixties, held titles like editor and publisher for various print publications during the seventies, was promoted to vice president of Moody Publishing in the mideighties, and became a full-time freelance writer in 1990. And now, as they say (whoever *they* are), the rest is history.

Like Jerry, my dad had a humble start. He was a country boy from Littles, Indiana, a fitting name for a town with about twenty-five people. Dirt roads were more common than paved ones, and local businesses had names like Earl's Restaurant and Hardware. My dad's father worked on the Whirlpool assembly line, and his mom was a homemaker. They had two boys, a pickup truck, and an outhouse. That is, until my dad built an indoor bathroom for the family at the ripe old age of twelve.

Dad left home at eighteen, first for college, then to sing in and manage a gospel group. He was hired as a youth pastor in the early seventies and was later promoted to director of ministries. He became a fund-raising consultant for churches nationwide in the mideighties and president of the same company five years later.

Then life took a bad turn. In the summer of 1991, my dad's

parents and only brother were killed by a drunk driver. A year later, after a fallout with his company's founder, he resigned from the business he'd helped build. And at the age of forty-two, my dad had to start over.

He took the little money he had and started his own business— a Christian bookstore, which was beautiful, thanks to my mom. It was small and quaint, and customers loved it. No one around offered the service they did, seven days a week. Dad was often in the store sunup to sundown.

But it didn't go well. My parents worked tirelessly for twelve years. There were long hours and precious few days off, and although there were moments when it seemed the store might find its footing, setbacks became commonplace. Mainstream chains like Walmart started carrying Christian products. Sam's Club offered bestsellers at half the price. Online shopping became the new rage, and most mom-and-pop stores just couldn't compete.

In 2005, exhausted and bankrupt, my dad was forced to close up shop. In the days that followed, when I asked how he was faring, he told me he was a failure. And that's pretty much all he said.

My dad's story really tears me up, and I've struggled to understand it. Why has life been so hard for him? Why do some people thrive while others seem to labor in vain? I love my father-in-law, and I'm thankful for his success. I've had a ringside seat to his incredible generosity, and by that I mean he gives away over half of what he earns to people and organizations in need—quite often anonymously. But my dad's a good guy too. He's smart, compassionate, and probably the hardest-working person I'll ever know. And he's obedient. In the face of personal tragedy and financial hardship, he has walked the Christian talk. So I can't help but wonder: *Where's the reward?*

TROUBLE WITH THE STASH

Sadly, it's not just my dad's happiness I'd like to buy. The truth is I really like money. The mall is one of my favorite places to spend an afternoon. My idea of a good time is thumbing through a Pottery Barn catalog. And Target? Well, let's just say *Tarjay* is a vile temptress.

Of course, everyone knows money can't buy happiness. Yet I pine for better clothes, area rugs, and seasonal candles. I can't wait until we get the kids new bunk beds, and the outside of the house needs to be painted. Oh, and there's the high-def TV and bookshelves for the family room, and I could really use a better digital camera. Heck, I even like buying toiletries. Just give me a store, a list, and a Diet Coke, and all is right with the world.

> *Everyone knows money can't buy happiness. Yet I pine for better clothes, area rugs, and seasonal candles.*

And just in case I sound shallow, there's a whole list of things I'd like to do for other people—if only I had the money. I've often imagined what it would be like to buy a car for a needy family or pay off a friend's school loan. I'd love to make significant contributions to our favorite charities and invest in the construction business my brother-in-law would like to start.

Yeah, money would be great for so many things, but my desire for it gets me into trouble. I get anxious. I overspend. I strategize how to get more. And all my pining leaves me discontent and unable to appreciate the things I do have. So I'm a mixed bag. I wish financial success for my dad because I love him and I want his life to be easier. I'd like to make a lot of people's lives easier. And I wish I had more money because I want more stuff. I guess I'm part noble, part greedy, and probably altogether misguided.

BAIT AND SWITCH

Four years ago we remodeled our house. We tore down walls, making three small rooms into one spacious family room. We redid the kitchen and the bathrooms, added a laundry room, and put in hardwood floors. I didn't care that we couldn't afford to decorate and furnish it completely, because it was adorable and it smelled new, which was good enough for me—for about six months.

I was content in my new house until I wasn't. Eventually I wanted new furniture. I wished I'd chosen a darker shade of ecru in the living room, and as the kids grew, our spacious room started feeling less spacious. And that's not the only time I've experienced fleeting thankfulness. I loved our new car until I realized we needed better gas mileage (can I get an "Amen!"?). I owned the perfect pair of boots until I realized, "Oh my gosh, this heel is so last season." I was happy with my refrigerator until I saw the one with the bottom freezer drawer.

And so it goes.

Because just as God says, money—along with all the stuff it can buy—doesn't satisfy. It's never enough.

> *Whoever loves money never has enough;*
> *whoever loves wealth is never satisfied with their income.*
> *This too is meaningless.*
> ECCLESIASTES 5:10

Last week I saw an ad for *The Real Housewives of Atlanta*, a reality show that follows a handful of women as they juggle their socialite schedules and highfalutin lifestyles. One of them actually said, "If I die tomorrow, I'm going to die wearing Dior." Gag. The quote makes for a great sound bite, but the truth is that when she dies in Dior, her body will rot in Dior, just like everybody else's. Because money doesn't put us in control of our lives; quite the contrary . . . it enslaves.

*No one can serve two masters. Either you will hate the one
and love the other, or you will be devoted to the one and
despise the other. You cannot serve both God and money.*

MATTHEW 6:24

We can serve God, or we can serve money, and we're allowed
to take our pick. And I'm pretty sure I've been serving money.
While I hate how that sounds, the evidence of my allegiance is
overwhelming. Not only do I fixate on money and the stuff I want
to buy, but I've also hated watching my parents struggle. At times,
I've despised God's inaction, knowing he could change their circumstances if he wanted to. And over time, the apparent injustice
of it all made me really angry.

Yet deep down I believe what God says about money. Grief—
my own experiences confirm that money is not all it's cracked up
to be. I want to follow God with a whole heart. I want right priorities. But it's awfully difficult to shift my focus and release my love
of money—or more accurately, to be released from it. Freedom is
hard to imagine.

But there is a way.

CHOOSING PRESENCE

I recently read Larry Crabb's book *The Pressure's Off.* In it he says,
"It's harder to enjoy God than his blessings. Offer a young child the
choice of having Daddy present Christmas morning with no gifts
or having Daddy absent with a stack of gifts piled high beneath the
tree, and the child might choose the gifts." He goes on to say that
only a mature person would choose God's *presence* over *presents.*

What does that say about me? I long for the giant stack of
gifts—for myself and everyone else. I know God is supposed to be
enough, but what does that mean when those you love are going
through bankruptcy? Or worse, how is God enough for people

who are actually hungry? And in the first-world reality most of us live in, how do we escape the bonds of materialism? How do we begin to desire God more than the blessings?

I have no idea. But rest assured God does.

> *I know what it is to be in need, and I know what it is to have plenty. I have learned the secret of being content in any and every situation, whether well fed or hungry, whether living in plenty or in want. I can do all this through [Christ] who gives me strength.* PHILIPPIANS 4:12-13

No offense, Paul, but if you ask me, contentment is darn hard to muster. I tend to think good circumstances will lead to contentment—that if we work hard and earn more money, we can buy stuff and get content. But Paul says our circumstances are irrelevant. He learned the secret to being content in *every* situation.

So what's the secret?

Relationship. Paul said he learned contentment, in spite of being poor and hungry, because he could live through

If I chase after money to bring me security or comfort, no amount of it will suffice.

anything with Jesus by his side giving him the strength to do so. I've tried really hard to be content with what I have, but I've missed the point and contentment has eluded me. Satisfaction has nothing to do with what I have. If I chase after money to bring me security or comfort, no amount of it will suffice. God wants me to rest in Him, so I'm wired *by Him* to rest *only in Him.*

He's smart like that.

> *Come, all you who are thirsty,*
> *come to the waters;*

> *and you who have no money,*
> *come, buy and eat!*
> *Come, buy wine and milk*
> *without money and without cost.*
> *Why spend money on what is not bread,*
> *and your labor on what does not satisfy?*
> *Listen, listen to me, and eat what is good,*
> *and you will delight in the richest of fare.*

ISAIAH 55:1-2

What an incredible picture of contentment. I love that God offers a feast of goodness to us, even to those with no money—a feast that will satisfy and delight our souls. And I *am* thirsty because I've spent a lot of years loving money and drinking the salt water of materialism. I'd much rather stand next to Jesus and accept His offer of contentment—after all, He's referred to as "living water" and the "bread of life" because He permanently satisfies our deepest needs.

> *The more we love Him, the more willing we'll be to depend on His strength.*

So the solution to our love of money is simple: love Jesus more. The more time we spend with Him, the more we'll love Him. The more we love Him, the more willing we'll be to depend on His strength. And as we depend on His strength, the money chains that bind us will be broken. Our hearts were created for singular devotion, and in Jesus we'll discover a satisfaction known only to those who, like Paul, want in on the secret.

ALL'S WELL THAT ENDS WELL

When my dad was nine years old, my grandma gave birth to a third son, who lived for only a few minutes. In the way only a child could, my dad prayed for a new baby. And knowing his parents had very little money, he specifically asked that it wouldn't cost them anything.

Precious, right?

Lo and behold, shortly after the loss of his little brother, my dad's newborn cousin came to live with the family. His older siblings were ill, and the baby's immune system was too vulnerable to be exposed, so he stayed in my grandma's care until it was safe to go home. And little Gary (my dad) was convinced that his prayer had been answered. After all, they got a baby who didn't cost anything. It was an open-and-shut case.

Oh, to be so satisfied with God's provision—I'm struck by such a simple faith. Surely when my dad prayed that prayer, he was imagining a more permanent situation. And yet a little boy's request was inarguably heard and answered, his deepest longing met.

Fast-forward to today, and I'm happy to report that my dad's story didn't end in bankruptcy. Within a year of losing his business, he found a job that was a perfect fit, and shortly after being hired, he was promoted to division manager. He now has the corner office, complete with windows and cushy swivel chairs.

And his little girl doesn't worry about him anymore. Not because he's financially stable, which he is, but because my understanding of who God is has changed. Because God really is good, whether His children are in the midst of bankruptcy or blessing. He's good because He provides; He says He will. Even on their worst days, my parents had what they needed—not what they wanted, and certainly not what I wanted for them.

But God knows our need, which is ultimately to experience and know more of Him, and He gives Himself freely and generously. And constantly. I used to doubt His goodness, especially in the face of turmoil or tragedy—hence the real reason I wanted stuff. With it, happiness seemed like such a sure thing. I desperately wanted my dad's business to succeed, and I prayed faithfully to that end because I believed it was the only good solution. But God had a different plan. And while it remains a mystery to me that some are financially blessed and others are not, God offers Himself to everyone.

And He's enough.

CHAPTER 3

Recognition

OCTOBER 22

Job title: homemaker

Awards I've received in my life: 1

Number of things I'm really good at: 8

Number of people who know I'm really good at 8 things: 6

Resolve to finish this book and become rich and famous.

Will settle for finishing this book.

MISS THANG

When I was fourteen, Marissa Jaggars was the new kid in school. She was pretty and smart and had the kind of skin that looked tan all year—your typical "it girl." She was welcomed into our class by drooling boys and giddy girls, and she climbed the ranks of popularity with ease.

And from what I remember, she was in all the smart-kid classes. AP English, calculus, physics. She graduated among the top in our class and went on to medical school, which surely surprised no one.

I wasn't jealous of Marissa (I was far too self-involved), but I easily could've been. She was a good friend, and we were on the same competition cheerleading squad . . . only she was the captain.

And she was the captain of both the football squad and the basketball squad. Captain, captain, captain. And she was nominated for homecoming queen. And she had a tiny—dare I say perfect—waist.

My high school stats read differently. I was a gymnast but had to quit because of a back injury. My first attempt at cheerleading landed me on the junior varsity squad, while most of my friends were already on varsity—they won state that year. When I joined the team the following season, we came in third at every competition. My academics took a similar path. Halfway through my sophomore year, I decided I wanted better grades, so I worked hard and did well. So well, in fact, that my guidance counselor nominated me for a national "Most Improved Student" award. I think the only thing worse than being nominated for the most-improved award is not winning it.

When I went to college, I decided things were going to be different. I studied all the time and got fantastic grades for the first two years. But then I met my future husband and started spending fewer hours in the library. Come graduation, my GPA was—and I'm not kidding about this—.001 below the number necessary to receive honors. I was told no exception could be made. My graduation pictures with my cap and gown *minus* that rope thingy around my neck still bug me.

As much as I hate to admit it, the lack of recognition I've received over the years bothers me. And while I might not have been jealous of Marissa in high school, I now wish I had a similar list of accomplishments to revel in—something more to put on my life's résumé. And although I generally like who I am and I enjoy being a stay-at-home mom, the truth is that laundry and PTA fund-raisers aren't as interesting as the day-to-day goings-on of a surgeon, at least according to *Grey's Anatomy*. It would be nice to be known for something so impressive. Which explains my affinity for the impossible—or, as I've come to know them, my *est* words.

COMING TO TERMS WITH *ISH*

Marissa wasn't my only fabulous friend. When it came to my circle in high school, Jill was the prettiest, Janet was the wittiest and the richest, and Cindy was the nicest. Gretchen had the cutest car—a tiny purple Jeep that looked like something Barbie would drive—and Sarah had the best hair. Robin was the sportiest (is that a word? athleticest?), and Katie was the goofiest, which made everything we did more fun.

And the way I saw my friends is the way I'd like to be seen. To be thought of as the bravest or the wisest. To be recognized for having the cleanest house and the best-behaved kids (which would make me the best mom, right?). I want my husband to think I'm the sexiest, my mom to think I'm the kindest, and my friends to think I'm the funniest.

> *I want my husband to think I'm the sexiest, my mom to think I'm the kindest, and my friends to think I'm the funniest.*

I want to be known.

Problem is, I'm none of those things, because my attributes are far more *ish* than *est*. I'm thinnish, but my metabolism slowed down a decade ago, and I love bread. I'm bravish, I think, though my only real gauge has been my willingness to go on scary roller coasters. My house is orderly, but dust bunnies are my constant companions. I'm smartish, but if I'm on your team in Trivial Pursuit, I assure you we'll lose. The bottom line is that I'm normal, in spite of all my efforts to hide it and all my goals to the contrary.

And I'm worn out. I don't want to define myself by what I do, but I can't seem to help it. Which begs the question: Why do I care what other people think? With all the pressure to accomplish and achieve status and be impressive, is it possible to believe I'm special simply because God says I am?

Beats me.

PARIS, MARTHA, AND ME

When it comes to helping us see our worth, God has a strategy.

> *As Jesus and his disciples were on their way, he came to a village where a woman named Martha opened her home to him. She had a sister called Mary, who sat at the Lord's feet listening to what he said. But Martha was distracted by all the preparations that had to be made. She came to him and asked, "Lord, don't you care that my sister has left me to do the work by myself? Tell her to help me!"*
>
> *"Martha, Martha," the Lord answered, "you are worried and upset about many things, but few things are needed—or indeed only one. Mary has chosen what is better, and it will not be taken away from her."* LUKE 10:38-42

I get Martha. Grief, I *am* Martha. She worked hard and stayed busy. She was a planner, and she was stressed. There was so much on her list of things to do that she wasn't able to spend time with Jesus. It's easy to judge her, but I imagine her motivation was similar to what mine would've been if Jesus and all His friends were coming over—to put on a good show. To be the best homemaker in town. Or *any* town. To impress. I'll bet she spent a lot of time cleaning before He came. I'll bet she lost a little sleep planning the meal. I'll bet she wanted everything to be perfect.

Mary, on the other hand, was chillin'—a state of mind I find fascinating and foreign. She wasn't concerned with logistics or with her reputation as a homemaker or with her sister's wrath. She just sat and listened to Jesus, and hers was the choice Jesus preferred.

I wonder what Mary got to hear Jesus say while Martha was in the kitchen. For that matter, I wonder what I miss when I'm busy with my lists. I wonder what Jesus thinks of the things I do to impress people (I have a hunch He's not a fan), and I wonder what my days would look like if I were more like Mary.

> *Jesus said, "Come to me, all of you who are weary and carry heavy burdens, and I will give you rest. Take my yoke upon you. Let me teach you, because I am humble and gentle at heart, and you will find rest for your souls. For my yoke is easy to bear, and the burden I give you is light."* MATTHEW 11:28-30, NLT

Interestingly, Jesus doesn't say that weary, burdened people should caffeinate to accomplish more or that they should rest more. Instead, He invites us to come to Him, and when we do, He provides us with rest. Because while we can choose to rest our bodies, *soul rest* only happens at the feet of Jesus. When we lay down our agendas, our focus shifts to *His* agenda. And in my experience, His agenda usually includes the reminder that I'm loved already. That He accepts me as I am, without title or accomplishment. That I don't need to seek approval from other people, because I'm worthy in the eyes of the only one who matters.

His rest is the kind that causes worry, insecurity, and desire for recognition to fall away, allowing us to fix our eyes on Him—and rightly so. After all, it wasn't Martha's cooking that was written about in history books. It was the Man she invited to dinner.

> *Don't let the wise boast in their wisdom,*
> *or the powerful boast in their power,*
> *or the rich boast in their riches.*
> *But those who wish to boast*
> *should boast in this alone:*

> *that they truly know me and understand that I am the LORD*
> *who demonstrates unfailing love*
> *and who brings justice and righteousness to the earth,*
> *and that I delight in these things.*
> *I, the LORD, have spoken!*
> JEREMIAH 9:23-24, NLT

I know a guy who has been a kung fu master for thirty years—he could walk down the streets of Compton with hundred-dollar bills hanging from his pockets without fear. He speaks eight languages and has traveled the world. He has a master's degree in clinical psychology, and he's currently working toward his doctorate. He's a dedicated family man and has raised three of the happiest, most respectful kids I've ever met (with the help of his fabulous wife, of course). And for the past twenty years, he's been a church planter and pastor.

Pretty unique résumé, though I don't often hear him mention it. Instead, he mostly talks about how God saved him from a life of sin and has shown mercy every day since; how the Lord grants wisdom and guidance, and loves us beyond what we can fathom. Because my kung fu friend knows that the stuff he's good at pales in comparison to the stuff God's good at.

And that there's only one thing worth bragging about.

> *You are all children of God through faith in Christ Jesus.*
> *And all who have been united with Christ in baptism have*
> *put on Christ, like putting on new clothes. There is no longer*
> *Jew or Gentile, slave or free, male and female. For you are*
> *all one in Christ Jesus. And now that you belong to Christ,*
> *you are the true children of Abraham. You are his heirs, and*
> *God's promise to Abraham belongs to you.*
> GALATIANS 3:26-29, NLT

Paris Hilton is a household name because she's an heiress to the Hilton Hotels empire. She spends her days shopping and her nights walking red carpets, but her fabulous life wouldn't exist if her name were Paris Smith, because her power is in her name—or more accurately, in her father's name.

The things I've allowed to define me, like my accomplishments (or lack thereof), become meaningless in light of my spiritual status.

And the same is true for me. In Christ, I have new clothes—a new identity. I have inherent value because of who my Father is, and I'm an heir in His family. The things I've allowed to define me, like my accomplishments (or lack thereof), become meaningless in light of my spiritual status. And while it's still difficult for me to imagine my life without the pressure to impress, in Jesus, it's mine for the taking.

THE ORIGIN OF SHINE

My favorite children's book is *You Are Special* by Max Lucado. Throughout my parenting years, I've read it over and over—and occasionally I even read it to my children. It tells the story of Punchinello, a wooden boy who lives in a land of wooden people called Wemmicks. If a Wemmick is talented or beautiful or smart, he is rewarded by other Wemmicks with a gold star sticker. If not, he's given a gray dot sticker. Every day they mark each other, and all the wooden people walk around covered in stars or dots or both.

Sound metaphorically familiar?

Poor Punchinello is the gray-dot type—average looking and talentless. One day he meets a Wemmick who has no marks, and when Punchinello asks her how it's possible to be stickerless, she tells him to visit Eli, the wood-carver, to find out.

When Punchinello meets his maker, Eli of course notices all the bad marks—but he doesn't care. He tells his little wooden creation that he *is* special and that the other Wemmicks don't know what they're talking about. The best part goes like this:

> *"Me, special? Why? I'm not very talented and my paint is peeling. Why do I matter to you?"*
>
> *Eli spoke very slowly. "Because you're mine. That's why you matter to me."*

Eli goes on to explain that for Punchinello to feel good about himself, he must spend time with his maker—every day—where he'll be reminded again and again that he's cared for and loved already. And then the stickers will fall off.

Of course, the same is true for me.

And, apparently, for Paul.

> *In order to keep me from becoming conceited, I was given a thorn in my flesh, a messenger of Satan, to torment me. Three times I pleaded with the Lord to take it away from me. But he said to me, "My grace is sufficient for you, for my power is made perfect in weakness." Therefore I will boast all the more gladly about my weaknesses, so that Christ's power may rest on me. That is why, for Christ's sake, I delight in weaknesses, in insults, in hardships, in persecutions, in difficulties. For when I am weak, then I am strong.*
>
> 2 CORINTHIANS 12:7-10

Something in Paul's life plagued him, and he asked God to remove it—a few times. But God *didn't* remove it, which seems harsh considering how dedicated Paul was to spreading the gospel and whatnot. Paul's response, however, was surprising, because while most of us work hard to self-promote and hide our shortcomings, Paul decided to talk his up—to delight in them.

Why?

Because the moon doesn't shine—that's why. In fact, the glow of the moon is actually the light of the sun reflecting off the moon's surface. Without the light of the sun, the moon would be dark. And the same is true with us and God. Our talents, our knowledge, our ability to love and laugh and weep and sing are mere reflections of who God is. He's the Light—the creator of all that's good and worthy of recognition. The only one who deserves the spotlight, which is obvious when we take the time to notice. And our weaknesses allow Him to shine in us all the more.

Our weaknesses allow Him to shine in us all the more.

I'm special because God says so, but *He's* the one worthy of attention and praise. Only at His feet will I have the ability to lay down my pursuit of perfection, along with my desire to be recognized for the eight things I do well. Only at His feet will I shine for the right reasons. And only there will I begin to see myself the way God sees me, which is the key to being okay with who I *really* am . . . *ish* words and all.

UNLIKELY SIGHT

Fanny Crosby is arguably the greatest hymn writer in history. More than eight thousand of her poems have been set to music, and more than one hundred million copies of her songs have been printed. Her works include classics like "To God Be the Glory," "Blessed Assurance," and "Christ, the Lord, Is Risen Today"—just to name a few. Her extraordinary faith will forever be recorded in black and white—permanent inspiration for those of us lucky enough to sing her songs a century or so later.

But less known than her music is the fact that Fanny was blind. At six weeks old she caught a cold, and the wrong treatment was prescribed, which destroyed her sight completely. Later in life she

told her mother, "If I had a choice, I would choose to remain blind
. . . for when I die, the first face I will ever see will be the face of
my blessed Savior."

Amazingly, the things that made life less than ideal for Fanny
had no hold on her heart—and neither did her success—because
her love for Jesus and for *His* glory consumed her. She was grateful
and humble, full of joy, and confident that God's plan for her life
was good. Confident that God would use her for His glory in spite
of her weakness. Confident that the story of Jesus was lovelier than
anything else she could have put to paper.

And at His feet, she shined like the moon.

I am Thine, O Lord, I have heard Thy voice
And it told Thy love to me;
But I long to rise in the arms of faith
And be closer drawn to Thee.

Oh, the pure delight of a single hour
That before Thy throne I spend,
When I kneel in prayer, and with Thee, my God
I commune as friend with friend!

Draw me nearer, nearer blessed Lord,
To the cross where Thou hast died;
Draw me nearer, nearer, nearer blessed Lord,
To Thy precious, bleeding side.

FROM "I AM THINE, O LORD"

CHAPTER 4 ⁞⁞⁞⁞⁞⁞⁞ # Relationships

NOVEMBER 23

Years married: 13½

Children: 3

Date nights this month: 1

Expectations for my husband: out the wazoo

Resolve to spend quality time with my husband after the kids go to bed, while also folding laundry and watching the season premiere of 24.

PRINCE CHARMING

My husband, Dallas, is a total catch—and not just because he's tall, dark, and handsome. He's one of the smartest people I know, not to mention one of the funniest. He's talented, confident, and articulate. He loves God, loves kids, loves people, and loves dogs. He's passionate about doing what's right and is always merciful, constantly extending grace and the benefit of the doubt. He's steadfast, trustworthy, and creative. He dreams big and works hard. And he's got a great butt.

Yep, when it comes to men, I hit the jackpot.

I remember the first time I saw him. I was sitting with friends in the middle of the cafeteria on our college campus, which was busy with chatter and eating. Enter Dallas. He walked past our table and, I swear, all the noise of the room dropped out. I sat staring. When he was out of sight—and I came to—my friends filled me in on who he was, which included who his girlfriend was.

Shoot.

The following year we had a few classes together, and group projects led to a genuine friendship, all shock and awe aside. For reasons *unrelated* to me (that's my story, and I'm sticking to it), Dal and his girlfriend broke up. And shortly after, we began dating.

It was a classic college romance. For two years, we took walks by the lake, studied together, and ate most of our meals together, all the while keeping a lookout for discreet places to make out (which on a small Christian campus was no easy task). And then Dallas proposed. We got married a few weeks after graduation, surrounded by our family and closest friends. It was a simple and beautiful wedding—a perfect start to forever.

But a perfect start does not a perfect relationship make. Because in spite of our lovely story, and as every married couple knows, reality finds us all.

FAIRY TALES AND FICTION

My two little girls love princess movies, and who doesn't? A beautiful, optimistic, animal-friendly maiden is swept off her feet by a dashing, romantic, fears nothing, withholds nothing prince. Of course, the two live happily ever after, consumed by a love that never waivers or fades. The honeymoon lasts forever, and wishes come true.

Our family's current favorite is *The Little Mermaid*. I love the part when Prince Eric resolves to find the beautiful stranger who saved him from drowning and marry her. After all, she sang to him, and her voice sounded really good.

Of course, we all know fairy tales are silly. Romantic, yes, but beyond unrealistic. Unfortunately, reality is often less exciting. I remember the early days of our relationship, when Dallas could do no wrong and I was content to just be with him. But thirteen years and three kids later, I'm not as easy to please. And that's not a criticism of Dal, because he's the same great guy I married. It's a criticism of my expectations of him and of marriage.

I want to be swept off my feet—the first day and every day. I want to be cherished, protected, and adored, like Elizabeth in *Pride and Prejudice*, Allie in *The Notebook*, and Bella in *Twilight* (don't judge me). At the very least, I want my needs met, which unfortunately for my husband, change by the day. Sometimes I need advice; other times empathy. Sometimes I need company; other times I need to be alone. Sometimes I need to cuddle; other times I need sex. Sometimes I need the garbage taken out; wait—that one never changes.

My poor husband. Fairy-tale maidens aren't nearly so high maintenance, and they never complain, which is impressive considering all the wicked spells and cleaning they endure.

And I wish I were more like them. Or maybe I wish my husband were more like Prince Charming. Truthfully, no matter how hard Dallas tries, there are times when he's not enough. I'm so thankful for him—my marriage is healthy and strong. But Jerry Maguire's "You complete me" doesn't quite ring true, because my husband isn't perfect, can't read my mind, and like me, doesn't always do the right thing.

I want to be swept off my feet—the first day and every day. I want to be cherished, protected, and adored.

Case in point (and I share this story with his permission), a year into our marriage, Dallas was caught looking at online porn at work. Talk about shattering the "perfect man, perfect marriage" facade. I was devastated and unforgiving for longer than I care to admit—but looking back, I realize I was more upset about the stain it put on our marriage than the actual offense. Men are visual, and their eyes are prone to wander—that wasn't new information. But I hated having a less-than-perfect track record. I hated being married to the wayward guy because I thought it was a reflection on me and my imperfection—like I wasn't pretty enough or interesting enough to keep his attention, and now other people might think so too. I became more concerned with damage control and protecting our reputation than my husband's well-being, more intent on recovering quickly for the sake of public opinion than on getting our marital car out of the ditch.

Thankfully, I'm married to a guy who couldn't have cared less what other people thought—he just did the work of getting back on track. He repented, got himself into an accountability group, earned my trust back, and now helps other men do the same. He's an open book (awful pun intended), he's humble, and he fixes what's broken. He's amazing, really, which made it easy to put him right back on the relationship pedestal, once again responsible for meeting my needs and living in the land of *perfect* portrayed on the big screen.

And expecting marital bliss is only part of the problem.

Growing up in the church, I was told that God should be my "first love," and I believe God *is* love. But there's a chasm between what I believe about God and what I've experienced of Him. God's presence isn't always palpable. He doesn't dialogue with me about my problems or offer situation-specific solutions. I can't hear His voice in the usual way or feel His touch, and to that end, I usually prefer people.

So when it comes to relying on loved ones, how much is too much? Since I've given first place in my heart to my husband (and my kids and my friends, for that matter), how do I fix it? How do I put God first in my love line? And for everyone's sake, how do I put aside Hollywood's depiction of what love looks like and get excited about things like sacrifice, "for better or worse," and Christ's sufficiency?

I don't know. Seems easier to watch a movie.

PROVERBIAL CRUMBS

The holidays have kept me busy, and I haven't had time to write. I haven't had time for a lot of things, including spending time with God. And for me, that's true to form. There've been no recent disasters, and there's no visible doom on the horizon. At the moment, life is smooth—and when life is smooth, I talk to God less. I think about God less. Bad habit, considering that He's supposed to be my most important relationship and that when it comes to our intimacy, He follows my lead.

> *Come close to God, and God will come close to you. Wash your hands, you sinners; purify your hearts, for your loyalty is divided between God and the world.* JAMES 4:8, NLT

So true—I am divided. As a wife, a mom, and now a writer, I struggle to make time for God, though I usually make time for everyone (and everything) else. I spend the day surviving my lists of errands and chores, some necessary but many self-imposed by my constant pursuit of perfection. I juggle the kids, their schedules, their homework, and their general neediness. I return calls from friends and my mom, and I try to stay caught up on e-mail and Facebook. I work on projects in every spare moment, whether writing or decorating another room (which usually means *re*decorating another room). And after the kids go to bed, it's Dallas time, which is when we watch TV, talk, cuddle, and catch up on the day. We wind down. When our shows are over and the kitchen is clean, I drag myself to bed, where I'm asleep in roughly two minutes.

Clearly God is often an afterthought. Or an absent thought. When I do sit down to spend time with Him, I often zip through my Bible study, filling in the blanks as fast as I can so that "time with God" can be checked off my list. I throw up prayer requests and forget to praise. I get to church on time but make mental to-do lists during the service. In truth, I plan most of my days without consulting the one who made the sun come up. I say I'm a Jesus follower, but I often operate like He's an intrusion to my productivity.

If I were God, I'd break up with me.

Obviously, relationships don't survive—let alone grow and thrive—under such neglect. But our immediate-gratification, fast-food culture has conditioned me to try to get the most done in the shortest amount of time—which works well for laundry, but it sabotages my walk with God. Because when I don't draw near, neither does He.

Yet in spite of my failure to put Him first, God has blessed me with people, because relationships are part of His design for our lives.

> Two are better than one,
>   because they have a good return for their labor:
> If either of them falls down,
>   one can help the other up.
> But pity anyone who falls
>   and has no one to help them up.
> Also, if two lie down together, they will keep warm.
>   But how can one keep warm alone?
> Though one may be overpowered,
>   two can defend themselves.
> A cord of three strands is not quickly broken.

ECCLESIASTES 4:9-12

God made the first woman, Eve, because "it is not good for the man to be alone" (Genesis 2:18). Jesus said we are to love our neighbors *and* our enemies, and to pray for those who persecute us (Matthew 5:44). God designed marriage to be the earthly representation of Christ's relationship with His church (Ephesians 5:21-33). The Bible says children are a gift from God (Psalm 127:3, NLT). And God wants us to have strong friendships that carry us through our hardest times (Proverbs 17:17).

But relationships suffer when God is benched. Left to my own devices, I lose my temper, I'm selfish, and I keep a good-size record of other people's wrongs (especially Dallas's). On the contrary, when I'm consistently spending time with God, I'm more self-controlled, generous, forgiving, thankful, and (on a really good day) gentle. Dallas and I are partners, but with God at the center, we're actually good at it. And when I'm in step with the Lord, my expectations for my husband, my marriage, and myself begin to line up with His.

> *One of the teachers of religious law . . . asked, "Of all the commandments, which is the most important?"*
>
> *Jesus replied, "The most important commandment is this: 'Listen, O Israel! The LORD our God is the one and only LORD. And you must love the LORD your God with all your heart, all your soul, all your mind, and all your strength.' The second is equally important: 'Love your neighbor as yourself.' No other commandment is greater than these."*
>
> MARK 12:28-31, NLT

Notice that Jesus doesn't mention butterflies or grand gestures—He just tells us to love God first and to love others as we love ourselves. Simple and beautiful, yet diametrically opposed to the modern-day relationship, where everyone seeks his or her own good and happiness. But the rising divorce rate, along with every episode of *The People's Court* and *Jerry Springer* (just to name a few) are evidence that happiness seeking doesn't make for strong, sustained relationships. Because happiness is temporary.

The perfect and happy beginning inevitably turns into the less exciting middle, where everyone's flaws are exposed. And if our priorities are out of whack, satisfaction in a relationship flies away with the butterflies. The bottom line is I'm a sinner in relationship with other sinners, and there's nothing perfect about that. But Jesus gave us the formula for relational success: we weren't meant to be each other's everything. We were meant to find our satisfaction in Jesus and His total sufficiency, and to love others in a way that displays how much we're loved already.

We were meant to love others in a way that displays how much we're loved already.

> *My God will meet all your needs according to the riches of his glory in Christ Jesus.* PHILIPPIANS 4:19

God is the source of, well, everything I need—and I believe it. But rearranging my relationship hierarchy, exchanging those who are seen for the promises of the one who is unseen?

Therein lies the challenge.

THE REAL THING

Two months ago my dad had a cardiac arrest. He spent the following week unconscious in the ICU, hooked up to more tubes than I could count. My family gathered around him, waiting to see if he would wake up. We didn't know if he'd be able to breathe again on his own. If he'd need open-heart surgery. If there would be permanent brain damage.

And the waiting was painful. Losing my dad was an unbearable notion, but so was the possibility of him living with brain damage—a circumstance I was all too familiar with. Seven years ago a dear friend of mine was in a motorcycle accident. He survived, but because of brain trauma, he could no longer walk, feed himself, or clean himself. It was almost impossible to understand him when he spoke, and when he died last summer, he was a shell of the man he once was.

In my dad's hospital room, all the possible scenarios ran through my head. And although the people I depend on most were there with me, they couldn't help. They couldn't make my dad wake up or console my fears about what life would be like if he did.

But God was there too. And the picture that came to mind in Trauma Room 3 will forever be burned in my memory. It was of Jesus standing next to me, His arm wrapped tightly around my shoulders. As the hum of the respirator drowned out every other sound, we watched my dad together.

The LORD your God is in your midst,
A victorious warrior.
He will exult over you with joy,
He will be quiet in His love.
ZEPHANIAH 3:17, NASB

God is not a distant ruler—He's in the hospital room. He's in our homes. He's in our cars when we're driving the kids to school. He's with us in our happy moments, our boring moments, and our scary moments, and He's there whether we choose to acknowledge Him or not. How sad it must be for Him when we're too busy to notice, and how sad for us that we miss opportunities to experience more of life in His presence.

Because He's not like anybody else.

I am convinced that neither death nor life, neither angels
nor demons, neither the present nor the future, nor any
powers, neither height nor depth, nor anything else in all
creation, will be able to separate us from the love of God
that is in Christ Jesus our Lord.   ROMANS 8:38-39

Now that's fairy-tale love. I'm quite certain no human being
is capable of loving me more. God wants us to be in relationship with other people—to love in good
times and in bad; to be generous with our
time, patience, affection, and forgiveness;
and to pick each other up when we fall,
because that's how we're loved by God
every day.

God is not a distant
ruler—He's with us in
our happy moments, our
boring moments, and our
scary moments, and He's
there whether we choose to
acknowledge Him or not.

But the biggies—like our peace of
mind, self-acceptance, and joy—should be
rooted in our relationship with God and
God alone. His love is perfect. Permanent.
My apologies to Tom Cruise, but only
God makes us complete. My people will love me, surprise me, fail
me, and amaze me, and I'll do the same for them. But God won't
fail me. Not ever. He's not a bystander of my life; He's a guide, a
protector, an unwavering friend. And above all, He's worthy of my
best love. Only when I love Him first will I experience, not just
believe, that He is who the Bible says He is.

He is love.

Dear friends, let us continue to love one another, for love
comes from God. Anyone who loves is a child of God and
knows God. But anyone who does not love does not know
God, for God is love.   I JOHN 4:7-8, NLT

HAPPILY EVER AFTER

For a year before our second child was born, I didn't talk to God much. In spite of my prayers to the contrary, my brother remained an adamant non-Christian, and my dad's business was on its last leg. As far as I could tell, God had checked out regarding the people I cared for the most, so I decided talking to Him availed little and wasn't worth my time.

In the midst of my apathy, little Maya arrived. For four months she slept in a bassinet by my bed, and every night God whispered in my ear while I stared at her. For four months, He quietly wooed me. For four months He told me that the way I feel when I look at my baby girl—the uncontainable love that gushes from my heart—doesn't compare to His love for me and for the ones I love.

I've been a passionate Christian for most of my life, but that doesn't mean I've always understood what it is to be in a passionate relationship with my Savior. On that front, I'm still learning. But I've tasted it and I want more. I want to know Him more. I want to be thankful for my loved ones every day, and I want to love them well. But I also want to hold them loosely, knowing that God is enough, should He ever have to actually be. And that my ultimate satisfaction, my happily ever after, is in Him.

(Fade to black; roll credits.)

CHAPTER 5 ||||||||| # Parenthood

Children: 3

Child-rearing fears: 16 and counting

Things I must control in order to keep my kids safe:

the whole wide world

Resolve to watch my kids every moment, visit the doctor religiously, and cook healthy foods; to prepare them for strangers, earthquakes, fires, and bullies; to always buckle them up and hose them down (tear-free, of course); to love them, encourage them, guide them, and pray for them; to avoid injuries, car wrecks, broken hearts, and bad guys; to practice what I preach; and to make the most of every teachable moment.

And to breathe.

BEANIE BABY

Elle Amanda (aka Beanie) is my four-year-old. She has dark brown eyes and a button nose—think Boo in the movie *Monsters, Inc.* She sings all the time and frolics more than she walks. She's sweet and she loves to snuggle. She makes up knock-knock jokes with every punch line the sound of a toot, and she has a fabulous, contagious laugh. She loves wearing dresses and dancing and pretending she's a princess. She's pure joy, and she adds light and life to our home every day.

She's a gift.

But raising her hasn't been easy. When Beanie was eighteen months old, we began to suspect something was wrong. She was too quiet. For months we assumed she was a late talker, but as time wore on, the words didn't come. Eventually we made an appointment with a speech pathologist, who confirmed our fears. Beanie had a significant developmental delay and would need to be evaluated for autism when she turned three.

Our hope was that with a year and a half of therapy under her belt, Elle would progress enough to rule out the diagnosis. But the language didn't come any faster, and odd behaviors emerged. Elle seemed unaware of things around her and often avoided eye contact with other people. She had an abnormally short attention span and didn't like crowds. She sought physical input by lying under mattresses and walking on her toes—not like a ballerina, mind you, but with her toes turned under completely, making her feet look like they were bent in half.

As feared, in the winter of 2008, Elle was diagnosed with autism, and our family grieved. Since early intervention is vital for autistic kids, we decided to add programs to her regimen. I'm thankful to report that during the past couple of years she has made tremendous progress, and we have reason to believe that she'll someday lead a normal life.

But we can't be sure. We can do all the right things, like keeping up with her therapy and trying special diets. We can provide her with the structure she needs to feel settled, and we can accommodate most of her quirks. But at the end of the day, we can't make Elle's brain work like everyone else's. I often wonder what the future will hold for her—if other kids will make fun of her or if boys will try to take advantage of her, if she'll graduate or get married or have children of her own.

Of course, there are no answers.

I suppose my questions aren't unique to Elle, though. Getting any child to adulthood happy and in one piece is a challenge because, as I've learned with Beanie, there are things I can't control—things that fall outside my jurisdiction. And my inability to be everywhere, every time, taking care of everything makes me worry, lose sleep, and squeeze.

MOMMY'S DEATH GRIP

As is true for most mommies, my children are my greatest treasure, and my goal in life is to mother them well. There's nothing I wouldn't do to keep them safe—be it beg, borrow, steal, or kill. My love for them is bigger than my ability to reason, and as such, I'm often at the mercy of my mommyhood. And so is everyone else.

My love for my kids is bigger than my ability to reason, and as such, I'm often at the mercy of my mommyhood.

I remember the first time our little family went out after Sam, our oldest, was born. We were walking the promenade in Santa Monica, watching street performers do their thing, when a dancer came by to collect donations. Intending to be funny, he reached toward Sam's stroller—you know, to get money from my baby, which got a chuckle from onlookers. But not from me. With slow-motion flare, I stepped in front of the stroller (which put me nose to nose with the poor guy) and said, "Nooooo!"

It wasn't my best moment. Luckily, after almost a decade of parenting, I now know the difference between a joke and actual danger. But my instinct to protect my kids at all costs remains, and it's the scenario we see time and time again—moms standing between their children and danger, fearless and empowered by relentless, crazy, ain't-nothing-gonna-hurt-my-baby love.

I love the story about a mom in California who was knocked to the ground by a stranger who then attempted to kidnap her child. I say *attempted* because Mom bounced up, chased down the ne'er-do-well, and saved her three-year-old. Which begs the question: Who in his right mind takes a child from his mother's arms? And then there was the mom in Florida who rescued her nine-year-old from an alligator. Apparently the kiddo was swimming in a lake near his home when a gator grabbed him by the legs—but not before his mother was able to grab hold of the boy's arms. Tug-of-war ensued, and Mom won. The little boy later told a reporter that in addition to the scars on his legs from the alligator, he had scars on his arms where his mother refused to let go. I have no idea whether that story is true or a fantastic urban legend, but it sounds right. Moms don't go down without a fight. And bad guys—be they man or beast—would be wise to take heed.

But while heroic mommy stories inspire me, I live in fear of things I can't control, because our world is scary. There are diseases I can't prevent and accidents I don't see coming. There's oral sex in elementary school, crystal meth, sexting, and other things I'm not hip enough to know about. There are school shootings and acts of terrorism. There are criminals of every kind and tragedies that happen every day. And, of course, there's autism. I'd like to think I'm tough enough to wrestle alligators and diligent enough to control who has access to my kids, that I have eyes in the back of my head, and that if I do my job right, Elle will find her voice.

But I'm beginning to know better.

So I have to wonder: Is there peace for a weary mommy? I know full well that I don't have the power to protect my kids all the time and that God is the only one equipped for the task. But how do I trust Him, knowing He may not choose to spare them the pain I work so hard to prevent? I spend my days checking off lists, believing that the things I do for my

My perfectionism has become hopelessly intertwined with my crazy mommy love.

children will prevent unnecessary heartache. And vice versa—that if I fail to be the best mom I can be, I will have failed *them*. And so, since my perfectionism has become hopelessly intertwined with my crazy mommy love, will I ever be able to say I've surrendered my children to God's will and care, and actually mean it?

I'm thinking, no.

NOCTURNAL JESUS

I often avoid watching the news. Stories of kidnapped or terminally ill children are usually too much for me to bear. I remember being really upset after watching a report on Natalee Holloway, the American teenager who disappeared during a graduation trip to Aruba. Dallas was out of town and I was alone, which should have been my cue to avoid all things tragic. But against my better judgment I watched, and true to form, I came unglued.

And I couldn't shake it. Watching Natalee's poor mother talk about her desperate, fruitless search for her child reminded me of how vulnerable my kids are, and how helpless I sometimes am to protect them. I called a friend, who did her best to talk me off the ledge. She gave me a few Bible verses to look at and encouraged me to pray and trust the Lord. I read Psalm 91 but refused to be comforted.

That is, until I watched *King Kong*. There's a part in the movie when Blondie runs away from the giant gorilla . . . and *into* a T. rex. She's a goner, for sure, but just before she gets eaten (this is a spiritual analogy, I swear), King Kong steps into the frame. And our heroine—recognizing her only shot at survival—slowly backs into the shadow of almighty Kong. Who, of course, wins the day.

And suddenly Psalm 91 came alive. Granted, it was an unconventional lesson, but it made the point. Because like the T. rex,

God is bigger than the scary stuff.

there are things I just can't handle alone—things with the power to consume me and my little people. I'm often told to not be afraid—that in the grand scheme of things, the odds of bad stuff happening are low. But minimizing the threat has never been a comfort. Only the image of God standing over me and my loved ones, covering us with His shadow, does the trick.

He's bigger than the scary stuff.

He who dwells in the shelter of the Most High
will rest in the shadow of the Almighty.
I will say of the LORD, "He is my refuge and my fortress,
my God, in whom I trust."
PSALM 91:1-2

God is bigger than the things that terrify me and bigger than my shortcomings, which is a good thing because much to my dismay, I'm not perfect. I make plans but can't see around corners. I get tired, and I can be impatient with my kids (most often around dinner-making time). I don't have all the answers, especially with Elle's ever-changing fixations and needs, so I make stuff up as I go along. And I'm terrified of snakes. No kidding. I'll throw down with anyone to protect my munchkins, but if a snake shows up in our backyard, it's every man (and small child) for himself.

Because in spite of my efforts to the contrary, I'm limited. God, on the other hand, is not. He watches over my children when I can't. He guards and guides their hearts. His judgment is never hindered by fear or anger or a lack of understanding. He's always merciful and always patient. He sees around the next corner—and the next and the next.

He's got it covered because He doesn't sleep.

> *My help comes from the LORD,*
> *the Maker of heaven and earth.*
> *He will not let your foot slip—*
> *he who watches over you will not slumber;*
> *indeed, he who watches over Israel*
> *will neither slumber nor sleep.*

PSALM 121:2-4

THE WORRY GENE

My son Sam is very conscientious—and by that I mean he worries too much. As I sit here writing, Elle is playing with our guinea pigs right next to me, and Sam is correcting her every move. And even though I've told him four times that I'm watching her, that they're not going to bite her, and that I'm in control of the situation, he remains unconvinced—to the point of tears. He thinks he knows how to care for Elle better than I do, which of course is ridiculous; I'm the mom and he's eight. If only he had a better understanding of his ability compared to mine. Surely then he'd be able to relax and go back to playing with his Star Wars figures.

And the irony is not lost on me. Because although Sam is driving me a little nuts, I have to acknowledge I'm just like him. Most days I think I can care for my children better than God can—that *I'm* the one who knows what's in their best interest; which is silly because, of course, the Maker is more equipped to determine what's best for *those He's made* than I am. And although He has placed Sam, Maya, and Elle in my care, a little humility on my part would allow me to relax, enjoy life more, and go back to playing with my Star Wars figures.

Or whatever.

> *Do not worry about your life, what you will eat or drink; or about your body, what you will wear. Is not life more than food, and the body more than clothes? Look at the birds of the air; they do not sow or reap or store away in barns, and yet your heavenly Father feeds them. Are you not much more valuable than they?* MATTHEW 6:25-26

I have to say—I worry a ton *and* I'm not a fan of birds (0 for 2). I live in LA, where the birds are so accustomed to people that they beg for food. Drop a crumb, and a dozen winged maniacs appear out of nowhere in full swarm.

Yet in spite of their bad manners and lowly place on the food chain, they're known and cared for by God. And if birds are, of course, so are we. I often justify my worry by believing it's rooted in my desire to parent well—that I'm preparing for the worst because that's what moms do. But a lot of my decisions are motivated by fear instead of wisdom, and my fear is propelled by my lack of faith that God is caring for my children well—which is illogical, as evidenced by His care for the birds.

Besides, worry doesn't work. I can't worry my children out of being hurt or lost or stolen. I can be attentive and responsible, teach them right from wrong, and prepare them for what may come. But worrying about what may come does nothing to prevent it. All worry does is allow fear to take up residency in my heart, poisoning my judgment and destroying my peace of mind.

I can't worry my children out of being hurt or lost or stolen.

God is in control, and He cares for and

watches over my children. Though I'll be the first to admit, His methods are sometimes unconventional.

> *Some time later God tested Abraham. He said to him, "Abraham!"*
>
> *"Here I am," he replied.*
>
> *Then God said, "Take your son, your only son, whom you love—Isaac—and go to the region of Moriah. Sacrifice him there as a burnt offering on a mountain I will show you."*
>
> *Early the next morning Abraham got up and loaded his donkey. He took with him two of his servants and his son Isaac [and] . . . set out for the place God had told him about. . . .*
>
> *Isaac spoke up and said to his father Abraham, "Father?"*
>
> *"Yes, my son?" Abraham replied.*
>
> *"The fire and wood are here," Isaac said, "but where is the lamb for the burnt offering?"*
>
> *Abraham answered, "God himself will provide the lamb." . . .*
>
> *When they reached the place God had told him about, Abraham . . . bound his son Isaac and laid him on the altar, on top of the wood. Then he reached out his hand and took the knife to slay his son. But the angel of the LORD called out to him from heaven, "Abraham! Abraham!"*
>
> *"Here I am," he replied.*
>
> *"Do not lay a hand on the boy," he said. "Do not do anything to him. Now I know that you fear God, because you have not withheld from me your son, your only son."*
>
> *Abraham looked up and there in a thicket he saw a ram caught by its horns. He went over and took the ram and sacrificed it as a burnt offering instead of his son. So*

Abraham called that place The LORD Will Provide. And
to this day it is said, "On the mountain of the LORD it
will be provided." GENESIS 22:1-3, 7-14

That story has always been hard for me. I'm horrified by God's
request of Abraham—and equally horrified by Abraham's compli-
ance. Sacrifice a child? What kind of God would demand such a
thing? And what kind of nut-job parent would obey? To be honest,
I'd like to put these verses into my "crazy things that happened in
the Old Testament and have nothing to do with me" file.

But I've heard modern-day stories, too, of parents with inexpli-
cable faith—moms and dads who've been able to look cancer and car
wrecks and unforeseen tragedy in the face and say with sincere hearts
that it's their duty and privilege to offer their children back to God.

And I'm perplexed by them. How is faith like that possible?
I can't imagine it. I can imagine never getting out of bed again
and, in Abraham's case, cursing God. But when it comes to my
children, I can't imagine saying, "Thy will be done" in the midst
of suffering and death.

Yet I know I have no control over when trouble comes. I want
to be a mom with unyielding faith and open hands. I want to rest
in God, knowing that He loves my children more than I do and
that His plans for their lives are good and right, come hell or high
water. I want to believe that the one who actually *did* sacrifice His
Son is worthy of my allegiance and trust. In my head, I know that
my children belong to Him already, and to live any other way is
to deny what *is*.

But believing it in my heart? Well, that's the trick, isn't it?

FLOCK DUTY

I fancy myself a really good parent—steady, loving, and wise. I give
my kids what they need and not what they don't. And if I'm all

that, surely God, the one who made me the way I am—the author of love and grace and generosity and wisdom—surely He's even more equipped to give my children what they need.

You parents—if your children ask for a loaf of bread, do you give them a stone instead? Or if they ask for a fish, do you give them a snake? Of course not! So if you sinful people know how to give good gifts to your children, how much more will your heavenly Father give good gifts to those who ask him. MATTHEW 7:9-11, NLT

I love that passage, and I mostly believe it. But when I see tragedy and suffering, especially in regard to children, I get all discombobulated. I'm a *why* child, only instead of asking why I have to eat my broccoli or why I can't take a bath with my remote control car, I want to know why God does the things He does. Especially why He allows children to suffer. Unfortunately, God doesn't usually explain Himself, and I'm left wondering what kind of God He really is.

Stick a pin in that. First, let's talk Hollywood.

I love the movie *The Lion, the Witch and the Wardrobe*—mostly because of Aslan, the mighty lion, who is both guardian and savior of the fantastical land of Narnia. Throughout the film we see the great lion leading and loving his followers to the point of sacrificing himself to save them. Though, like Jesus, he doesn't stay dead. My favorite lines come at the end, when Lucy and her faun friend, Mr. Tumnus, are watching Aslan leave Narnia. Their conversation goes like this:

TUMNUS. *Don't worry. We'll see him again.*

LUCY. *When?*

TUMNUS. *In time. One day, he'll be here, and the next, he won't. . . . After all, he's not a tame lion.*

LUCY. *No, but he is good.*

Not tame, but good. Rather counterintuitive, if you ask me. I usually equate safe and happy with good, and suffering with bad. And while God is often a safe haven from scary things, His plans are unpredictable, often include suffering, and frequently fall outside the comfort zone. In other words, He does things and allows things I wouldn't. And so, in order to trust Him, it's imperative for me to first believe He's good, in spite of (and in the midst of) not-so-good circumstances.

> *I am the good shepherd; I know my sheep and my sheep know me—just as the Father knows me and I know the Father— and I lay down my life for the sheep.* JOHN 10:14-15

What greater sign of goodness could I ask for than that Jesus, the Good Shepherd, would sacrifice His life for my children? I sometimes see the Cross in an exclusively corporate sense—Jesus died for all, which is absolutely true. But when I focus only on the "all" part, Christ's sacrifice becomes less personal. It's easier for me to trust Him when I remember He died for *my* children—that He laid down His life for Sam, for Maya, and for Elle. Nothing else is necessary to believe that He'll continue to act in their best interest. That He's good, not tame—as evidenced by the things He allows—but good nonetheless.

So why does the Good Shepherd allow suffering? Since Christ's death on the cross was to save us from suffering an eternity without Him, He clearly doesn't *want* us to suffer. He wants us in heaven with Him, though in the meantime (while we're waiting for eternity to commence), He allows us the freedom to make our own choices. And quite frankly, people make stupid, horrible, selfish choices, and kids are often the victims. While cancer and autism and an infinite number of ailments are not a result of bad choices, they're allowed by the one who made us, loves us, died for us, and waits patiently for us to accept His gift of life. They're allowed for reasons we don't get to know yet, but what we *can* know is that God's the good guy, the one who aches for our redemption, and the one who longs for restoration—for us, for our children, and for the world He made. And in His mercy, He brings good out of the mess in ways we could never even imagine.

We know that in all things God works for the good of those
who love him, who have been called according to his purpose.
ROMANS 8:28

I believe that God is good. Yet even on my most surrendered and trust-filled day, I still want stuff for my kids like health and happiness and a long life. But the thing I want even more is for them to know the Good Shepherd—the one who loves them more than I do. Since I've realized I have less power over my children's futures than I originally thought, and that God isn't necessarily going to grant my "well wishes" for my kids, I must acquiesce to a new strategy—God's strategy. In other words, good-bye to trying to be the perfect mommy, and hello to lots and lots and lots of prayer.

Do not be anxious about anything, but in every situation,
by prayer and petition, with thanksgiving, present your
requests to God. And the peace of God, which transcends all
understanding, will guard your hearts and your minds in
Christ Jesus. PHILIPPIANS 4:6-7

Good-bye to trying to be the perfect mommy, and hello to lots and lots and lots of prayer.

Last summer I met a couple with five children. The oldest was in his twenties, the youngest just thirteen. They were amazing kids—polite, thoughtful, chivalrous, well spoken, and smart. So smart that when we got lost on our way to my hotel, they were able to correct course by looking at the stars. I'm not kidding. We were lost and they looked at the stars, and then we weren't lost. I have no idea how it happened; I just know I made it back to my room safe and sound.

Since it doesn't get more impressive than navigating by way of stars, I asked their parents how they turned out five amazing, Jesus-loving kids. Their answer? Prayer, which at the time I thought was an annoying thing to say. I mean, all good Christians know we're supposed to pray for our kids. That's obvious. I wanted a strategy—something I could do to ensure my children would turn out okay. But in His mercy, God is teaching me that I'm weak and unable to make things turn out okay. And that while I'm far from perfect, I can entrust my precious children to the one who actually is perfect. When we start to grasp who we are and who God is, our recourse, indeed, becomes prayer. Desperate, frequent, begging, pleading, loving, thorough, faithful prayer.

It's possible to lead and love my children in the way they should go, but it's not possible for everything to work out according to my plan—heartache and suffering will most assuredly accompany the journey. Only in the arms of Jesus will I find peace, knowing my precious little people are well looked after. Only in the arms of Jesus will I be able to discern how to pray the prayers that need to be prayed. And only in the arms of Jesus will He change my heart, bringing me to the place where I can accept His sovereign will. I'll never be a perfect parent, but I'm learning to be a praying parent.

And I'm starting to feel relieved it's not all up to me.

NIGHTTIME

For the past six months, Elle hasn't slept well. She's had a difficult time falling asleep and often wakes in the middle of the night for hours at a time. At first Dallas and I had no idea what to do. Our parenting experience told us to be tough—to not jump up and go to her every time she cried, which would certainly cause Beanie to develop bad habits. But the waking up and staying up didn't stop, and as time wore on, I began to feel desperate.

I'll forever remember the time I went to her room around four in the morning. She'd been awake for two hours (as had I) and was crying. I knelt down next to her bed to plead with her to sleep, as I had many times before. Most nights I would say something like, "Daddy's sleeping, Maya's sleeping, Sammy's sleeping, and now Beanie needs to sleep." I thought if she understood what was supposed to be happening, she would get on board. But this was my fifth time up, and out of sheer frustration I said, "Beanie, what's going on?" She looked at me through tears and said, "Mommy, I'm broken."

My heart sank. Turns out she knew exactly what she was supposed to do but couldn't do it. Her little brain just wouldn't let her sleep. I curled up next to her, assuring her she wasn't broken, and we slept together the rest of the night as we have many times since. I've come to understand that even when she's struggling and can't fall back to sleep, my presence is a comfort to her.

And God wants to do the same for me. I'm going to struggle, and my kids are going to struggle. They will succeed and fail, laugh and cry, win and lose, and at some point experience brokenness. But there's a light at the end of every tunnel because while there are few things more awful than having to watch my children suffer, God is near. He's there to guide me as I guide them. He loves my kids, He's got a plan, and He is good.

Even when it's dark outside.

He will cover you with his feathers.
  He will shelter you with his wings.
  His faithful promises are your armor and protection.
Do not be afraid of the terrors of the night,
  nor the arrow that flies in the day.
Do not dread the disease that stalks in darkness,
  nor the disaster that strikes at midday. . . .

The LORD *says, "I will rescue those who love me.*
  I will protect those who trust in my name.
When they call on me, I will answer;
  I will be with them in trouble.
  I will rescue and honor them."

PSALM 91:4-6, 14-15, NLT

MARCH 21

Plans failed in recent years: 4

Plans currently in the works: 7 (including surviving being a
single mom while my husband shoots and edits two films, which
will hopefully sell well, allowing us to make enough money to pay
for an international adoption, move away from Los Angeles, and
buy a bigger home with a bigger yard in a better school district)

Resolve to work hard, save money, and create contingency plans.
Oh yeah—and to pray that God will direct our path.

OTHER PEOPLE'S BABIES

My friends Becky and Durrell have four kids under the age of
six. They've outgrown their house—three bedrooms and one
bathroom, made even smaller by the presence of a very large dog.
They've outgrown their Honda—watching them get out of their
five-seater reminds me of clowns emerging from a little car. They've
outgrown their closet space, their office space, their kitchen table,
and LA, which is why they're moving to Virginia, where square
footage will rise and the cost of living will fall.

It's not that having four children is an incredible feat in

itself—lots of people have large families. It's the whirlwind way their family grew that makes them unique. After completing graduate school, Becky moved from New York to Los Angeles to pursue her dream of being a screenwriter. Shortly after, she met Durrell (also an aspiring screenwriter), and the two married within a year. Then came Ben, with his blond hair, blue eyes, and tan skin—the perfect California baby.

And life was good.

But when Becky and Durrell decided it was time for a second kiddo, things didn't go as planned. Two miscarriages in one year made them wonder if being in their forties was affecting their baby odds. Not wanting to give up the dream of a bigger family, they attended a seminar on fostering to adopt, primarily for the purpose of getting information. Five days later (and contrary to the way the system usually works), eighteen-month-old Anthony was placed in their home. Three months after that, Sabrina was born and placed with her big brother. Six months after that, fertile-myrtle birth mom was pregnant again, and Lily makes four. All three siblings have been officially adopted, and Becky and Durrell have the large family they've always wanted.

But just in case it sounds like pretty smooth sailing, there's a catch, because Lily's doctor recently became concerned about her small head coupled with a few developmental delays—both symptomatic of fetal alcohol syndrome. When confronted with questions about her pregnancy, Lily's birth mom confessed to using crystal meth, which is often accompanied by alcohol. Terrified of what they might find, Becky and Durrell took Lily to a neurologist for an in-depth examination. Miraculously, the tests for FAS came back negative. Praise God, Lily showed no sign of any ailment connected with drug abuse in utero.

Her blood work, however, revealed something the doctors weren't looking for. Lily's sixteenth chromosome is duplicated, which means that in all likelihood Lily will be autistic. And while it's comforting to know her developmental delays are not the result of her mother's drug use—that Lily isn't a permanent victim of horrible choices—the road ahead remains uncertain and scary.

Amid the chaos of a fast-growing family and a looming disorder, nothing of significance has happened with regard to Becky's and Durrell's screenwriting. My friends have come close to making it through Hollywood's door but haven't quite. So to make ends meet, Becky writes company bios for coffee table books and Durrell does accounting work. Both continue to write in their spare time (ha), but their focus has shifted to raising their four children and doing everything in their power to help baby Lily.

Of course, Becky and Durrell love their children and are poised for the fight ahead, but it's certainly not the road they would have chosen ten years ago. Having to say good-bye to my dear friends as they leave for Virginia isn't exactly what I would have chosen either, especially considering Dallas and I are at the start of a very similar road.

STOP, GO, REPEAT

Since we were first married, Dallas and I have talked about wanting to adopt—some would say ad nauseam. When our daughter Maya was two, we decided to stop getting pregnant and start adopting. But within a short time (and just after I gave away my maternity clothes), I got pregnant with Elle and our plans were put on hold.

Fast-forward to Elle's second birthday, when we again decided the time was right to adopt. We chose an agency, a country, a gender, and a name. We went through a home study and filled out paperwork. But when it came time to submit our request to Thailand, Elle's behavior became more difficult to manage. Then came her official diagnosis of autism. We decided to put the process on hold a second time until we had a better handle on our daily routine and Elle was more settled.

A year went by.

By the time Elle was approaching four, we again felt ready. We submitted our application to Thailand and waited to hear back. But soon after, we were informed by Thailand's department of something-or-other that the country was stopping foreign adoptions and the only children available to us would be those with special needs.

Since we already have a child with special needs, I felt both uniquely qualified and totally overwhelmed. (Two, God? *Really?*) We considered the laundry list of potential issues and decided on the ones we could handle, which included a child with a cleft palate. Because of Elle, we're familiar with the world of speech therapy, not to mention we know a top plastic surgeon who agreed to do the surgery pro bono. Surely this was God's plan. It made perfect sense.

We resubmitted our application.

In spite of our enthusiasm and resources, the Thai board ruled that a cleft palate would be too much for us to deal with since we already have three children. They told us they would only approve a child with a minor issue, which (as you can imagine) wasn't horrible news. Of course, it didn't make sense—after all, we were willing and able. But it was a relief to know that any child we took in would have a treatable ailment, and hey, we'd shown we were willing to do the hard thing but wouldn't have to. A spiritual win-win, if you ask me.

But nine more months went by without a word from the board. So Dallas started another film, and the adoption once again faded into the background. Life was business as usual. That is, until nine days ago, when our world turned upside down.

HOLD THAT THOUGHT

The truth is, this has been a tough chapter to write because when nothing goes according to plan and everything is up in the air, circumstances and life lessons are darn hard to decipher. And the more detours and curveballs I face, the more I wonder, *What's the point of planning anything?*

I've heard it said, "Make your plans but hold them loosely." But the only plans I truly hold loosely are the unrealistic ones—like living in my dream home in Tuscany, surrounded by my family and closest friends. The things I *have*—my kids, my husband, my health, my goals—those I hold tight. So I can't help but wonder, *What's the secret to holding plans loosely?* And is that even possible for a type A control freak like me?

> *"I know the plans I have for you," declares the LORD, "plans to prosper you and not to harm you, plans to give you hope and a future."* JEREMIAH 29:11

When my parents were on the verge of bankruptcy, well-meaning believers would remind them of that verse, which of course made sense. It's encouraging and inspiring—a top 10-er, for sure. But after years of extreme financial struggle and no sign of relief, my mom grew weary of hearing it. She began to wonder what it really meant and how she was supposed to view her life in its light. Fed up (and more ticked off than curious), she decided to read the verse in context.

Turns out that *in context*, Jeremiah 29:11 isn't as feel-good as it's often thought to be.

> *This is what the LORD Almighty, the God of Israel, says to all those I carried into exile from Jerusalem to Babylon: "Build houses and settle down; plant gardens and eat what they*

*produce. Marry and have sons and daughters; find wives for
your sons and give your daughters in marriage, so that they
too may have sons and daughters. Increase in number there;
do not decrease. . . ."*

*This is what the LORD says: "When seventy years are
completed for Babylon, I will come to you and fulfill my good
promise to bring you back to this place. For I know the plans
I have for you," declares the LORD, "plans to prosper you and
not to harm you, plans to give you hope and a future. Then
you will call on me and come and pray to me, and I will
listen to you. You will seek me and find me when you seek
me with all your heart. I will be found by you," declares the
LORD, "and will bring you back from captivity. I will gather
you from all the nations and places where I have banished
you," declares the LORD, "and will bring you back to the
place from which I carried you into exile."*

JEREMIAH 29:4-6, 10-14

So, yeah, God had a plan for the Israelites. He took credit,
in fact, for allowing Babylon to conquer and force the Jews into
exile—which means He was the one who carried them away from
their land, their homes, their livelihood, and the Temple, which
was at the center of their religion and culture. God's people became
aliens in Babylon, ruled by a cruel king who demanded they worship his gods or be burned alive. And just
in case the Israelites weren't sure what to
do next, God told them to hunker down,
plant crops, get married, and make babies
because they were going to be there for
seventy years before finally going home.

> *One of the frustrating
> things about being a
> Christian is that we rarely
> get to know the reasons
> behind God's plans.*

That was the plan—the means by
which God would bring redemption,

hope, and a prosperous future to the Israelites. Not quite the same ring to it—in context, I mean. So what are we to conclude? Clearly Scripture speaks of God's love for His people, yet His plan for them allowed immense pain. He didn't explain why their suffering would last so long; He just told them what to expect.

To which I say . . . *eesh.*

DUMB IT DOWN

For me, one of the frustrating things about being a Christian is that we rarely get to know the reasons behind God's plans—which is why I appreciate stories (though there are few) that offer such insight.

> *As [Jesus] went along, he saw a man blind from birth. His disciples asked him, "Rabbi, who sinned, this man or his parents, that he was born blind?"*
>
> *"Neither this man nor his parents sinned," said Jesus, "but this happened so that the works of God might be displayed in him. As long as it is day, we must do the works of him who sent me. Night is coming, when no one can work. While I am in the world, I am the light of the world."*
>
> *After saying this, he spit on the ground, made some mud with the saliva, and put it on the man's eyes. "Go," he told him, "wash in the Pool of Siloam" (this word means "Sent"). So the man went and washed, and came home seeing.*
>
> *His neighbors and those who had formerly seen him begging asked, "Isn't this the same man who used to sit and beg?" Some claimed that he was.*
>
> *Others said, "No, he only looks like him."*
>
> *But he himself insisted, "I am the man."*
>
> *"How then were your eyes opened?" they asked.*
>
> *He replied, "The man they call Jesus made some mud*

*and put it on my eyes. He told me to go to Siloam and
wash. So I went and washed, and then I could see."*
JOHN 9:1-11

I love this guy's testimony—*I was blind and Jesus made me see.*
I have to admit, if I had been this man, blind since birth and now
miraculously healed, I would celebrate for a moment, and then I'm
pretty sure I'd ask Jesus why He'd waited so long to rescue me. I'm
ashamed to say it, but I always question the Lord's plans, even in
the presence of mercy and miracles.

I wish I weren't like that.

Thankfully for people like me, Jesus told His disciples that
the man was born blind so the works of God, through the healing
power of Jesus, would be displayed in his
life. Simple and to the point, and it makes
perfect sense. After all, if this story hadn't
been written on the pages of Scripture,
how else would we know that God makes
blind men see? If Christ hadn't demon-
strated His power, His compassion, and
His love through miracles (and ultimately
through His death and resurrection), how
would we know that He's *all about rescue*?
If it weren't for divinely ordered moments,
how would we know that God indeed has a specific plan for our
lives and that we're not at the mercy of a fallen world?

> *If it weren't for divinely
> ordered moments, how
> would we know that God
> indeed has a specific plan
> for our lives and that we're
> not at the mercy of a fallen
> world?*

We wouldn't.

But like I said, God doesn't always spell it out. And that's where
faith in *who* instead of *what* comes into play.

> *"My thoughts are not your thoughts,
>   neither are your ways my ways,"*

declares the LORD.
"As the heavens are higher than the earth,
so are my ways higher than your ways
and my thoughts than your thoughts."

ISAIAH 55:8-9

Those verses always make me think of the crazy dog my husband and I had when we were first married—long before *Dog Whisperer* was even a thing. The moment our dog was off leash, he'd run away. Far away. We chased that dog across streets, into neighbors' backyards, through Kentucky cow pastures, and once to the shore of a thinly frozen pond.

Xerxes (as in King Xerxes, which *so* suited him) clearly loved the ice under his paws and had no intention of getting off, in spite of Dallas's pleas from the water's edge. See, Dallas knew the ice was going to break any moment and that the best plan was to get off immediately. But Xerx was just a dog, interested only in what he thought he knew, and certainly not privy to the bigger picture.

And in case it's unclear, I'm the dog in this scenario. I think I know how things should be because after all, it's my life, my kids, my goals. But like Dallas with that crazy dog, my loving Father sees and understands things I don't, which makes it silly—reckless, even—to go my own way. Bottom line: God doesn't do stuff the way I do stuff, and my plans, though often well intentioned, consistently fall short of His.

So the question becomes, how do I make the right plans? I don't want to be a dog on the ice—I want to walk in God's will, ready for storms and sunshine, knowing He's the author of both and that His purposes have eternal worth. I want the things I do to make a difference, not just for me and my family, but for His Kingdom. But in the midst of a busy schedule full of school, therapy, soccer practice, playdates, and my husband's movie making, what does that mean? What does it look like to go God's way—to trust God's plan—instead of my own?

Well, that depends on the day.

THE PERKS OF SHEEP

Like I said, a little over a week ago Dallas and I received difficult news from Thailand. In spite of the board's previous decision to refer a child with only a minor medical issue, the little boy we were matched with had a condition that far exceeded what we thought we could handle. Our lives would be significantly changed by taking on such a challenge, and upon first hearing, I was paralyzed with fear.

But then I prayed. My people prayed. I confessed my fear and desire to go my own way. Check that—to *run* my own way, as fast as my feet could carry me. And God was gracious. He calmed my fears, steadied me with peace, and granted wisdom. He allowed me to see the situation clearly, to see this little boy the way He does and to love him. As a result, we decided to go forward in faith, believing God would equip us come what may, as long as we remained in Him and surrendered to Him in faith. He says He will.

> *Remain in me, as I also remain in you. No branch can bear fruit by itself; it must remain in the vine. Neither can you bear fruit unless you remain in me.*
>
> *I am the vine; you are the branches. If you remain in me and I in you, you will bear much fruit; apart from me you can do nothing.* JOHN 15:4-5

Last week I was *remaining*, and my load was lighter. Then God made a move I didn't see coming and is now requiring more. That's the thing about remaining: the very idea acknowledges adventure—the unknown we can count on when we're following instead of leading, the ride that chucks our perfect plans and our desire to control everything out the window. And as we follow, God produces fruit in us like peace, love, compassion, and supernatural strength, allowing us to be better than we were the day before. Allowing us to be more like Jesus.

> *Now listen, you who say, "Today or tomorrow we will go to this or that city, spend a year there, carry on business and make money." Why, you do not even know what will happen tomorrow. What is your life? You are a mist that appears for a little while and then vanishes. Instead, you ought to say, "If it is the Lord's will, we will live and do this or that." As it is, you boast in your arrogant schemes. All such boasting is evil.*
> JAMES 4:13-16

I used to say, "If it's God's will, we'll adopt" or "If it's God's will, we'll make another movie" or "If it's God's will, we'll move to a better school district or buy a bigger house," as if stating my plans correctly were the point. But James wasn't talking about semantics; he was talking about living life in surrender to God's plans. In other words, am I willing to switch gears for Jesus? Am I ready to embrace the things and people He puts in my path? Am I praying for wisdom, discernment, and the patience I need to wait on God?

The truth is, I don't remember praying much about our adoption until this past week. I guess I thought adoption was a good thing—a godly thing—and since we felt called to it, what else was there to pray about? We simply needed to march forward in obedience. Somehow it hadn't occurred to me to ask God about logistics, and now I can't help but wonder if we chased our tails for a few years because we didn't pray enough—because we didn't surrender our plan to God, well intentioned as it was.

*Ask and it will be given to you; seek and you will find; knock
and the door will be opened to you. For everyone who asks
receives; the one who seeks finds; and to the one who knocks,
the door will be opened.*

*Which of you, if your son asks for bread, will give him a
stone? Or if he asks for a fish, will give him a snake? If you,
then, though you are evil, know how to give good gifts to your
children, how much more will your Father in heaven give
good gifts to those who ask him!* MATTHEW 7:7-11

I used to think those verses were for people seeking Christ for
the first time. But I realize now, Jesus was telling *all* His followers
to ask. To seek God, His will, and His wisdom. To see Him as the
giver of good gifts and the things we need most. To trust that God
is as loving and good as He says He is, and to want more of what
He offers—whatever that may be.

To put a face on it, recently my husband heard Phil Vischer
(the creative giant behind VeggieTales and cofounder of Big Idea
Productions) speak at a conference. Vischer told of the rise and
financial fall of the company he'd worked so hard to build. How
he was once the man with a plan, always able to articulate an
answer to the "Where do you want to be in five years?" question.
But over time, and as a result of plans gone awry, he has come to
the conclusion that where he is in five years is none of his business. That it's up to God, and he's just along for the ride—which
is countercultural, to say the least. Almost everyone I know has
a five-year plan—we can't help it. To release our plans and leave
ourselves open to whatever God has in store is scary and feels
downright impractical.

But I want to surrender, not because, as many people say,
"God won't give you something you can't handle" (read the Bible;
that's just bad theology). Of course God gives us things we can't

handle—that way we'll get the heck out of the driver's seat. No, I want to surrender to God because, in His wisdom and holiness, He's a much better navigator than I am, and I'm willing to defer to His sovereignty, willing to walk a path unknown, believing He'll be faithful to lead me on it.

> *Of course God gives us things we can't handle— that way we'll get the heck out of the driver's seat.*

> *The LORD is my shepherd, I lack nothing.*
> *He makes me lie down in green pastures,*
> *he leads me beside quiet waters.*
> PSALM 23:1-2

Too often I see God as the taskmaster, always requiring the difficult thing, always demanding service and sacrifice and death to self. But while following Jesus isn't easy, mercy, peace, and rest transcend the hard parts, making them doable and granting unspeakable joy in the process.

Since the moment Dallas and I decided to move forward with the adoption, I've been resting. So much so that I'm starting to feel lazy—soul lazy, really. I'm not even sure *lazy* is the right word, but I have nothing else to compare my current state of mind to. I'm usually the anxious type, always considering what could go wrong and worrying it will—*and* working to fix things that haven't happened yet. But at the moment, I'm calm, collected, and waiting patiently for the details to work themselves out. I'm not fearless, but I'm no longer fearful. And when it comes to life-altering decisions, that's a first for me, because I haven't always seen God as the Shepherd. But this time, when my plans got changed, I lay down.

God is the Shepherd, tending to His flock—protecting,

I'm not fearless, but I'm no longer fearful.

providing for, and leading the sheep He loves. Now that I've experienced His rest, I'm not sure why I was so opposed to it before—why I spent time trying to fig-

ure things out on my own. No more, though. I'm done making "perfect" plans. Done with working so hard to maintain control, and done with the fear that sets in when I lose control. Instead, I'm going to pray more and surrender my wants and needs to the Lord. After all, He knows them already, and His plans for me are good. And so are His rest and peace and joy and hope.

SOMEDAY HOME

Funny how things work out sometimes. Or don't. Shortly after their cross-country move, Becky and Durrell joined forces with a Virginia-based nonprofit called Kids in Families (KIF), an organization that aims to inspire and facilitate the church to meet the needs of abandoned and at-risk children through fostering and adoption. They're planning to write and produce film projects for distribution in theaters, in churches, and on TV that promote their cause. In other words, God is merging their love for screenwriting with their passion and love for at-risk children. Watching the two come together is awe inspiring. Only God could do something like this.

Lucky for me, I have friends who demonstrate what it looks like to follow God and His crazy plans, friends who believe there's more to life than what they can see, friends who trust God with their hopes and dreams. And when my dear friends heard the news of our pending adoption, they responded with words that bring me hope as I wait for the day when I, too, will meet my son.

Amanda,

I got your e-mail, grabbed a milk bottle, rocked Lily, and started praying. I cried and prayed for you as I looked down at my little "imperfect one" and realized that it is the prayers of believers that have helped sustain me through our walk with her. I am praying for you now, with that same fervency.

It struck me as I rocked and prayed that there is nothing uncertain about our God. He is specific in all He does, and that includes the demeanor, personality, emotional makeup, and physicality of your little boy. Crazy how we can conjure up every scenario and then imagine how we would handle it, and then God gives us one so completely unimaginable—and we are back to the only solace: prayer.

As I've walked this road, I have come to realize I'm not a planner; I'm a hoper. I hoped I'd be married at twenty-six; I hoped I'd live in New York City; I hoped I'd work as a screenwriter; I hoped I'd have my first child at twenty-eight. I can't say I had a well-thought-out plan for any of these things (and a million others)—I just sort of aspired to them. Some of them have happened; some have not. But whether I refer to the stuff I want to happen in my life as plans, hopes, dreams, or whatever, at some point or another, plans fail, hopes defer, and dreams die. So then what? I'm face to face with God, my brow furrowed, saying, "What were you thinking?" And then I realize the real question is, What was I thinking? Thank God I didn't marry that guy at twenty-six, and thank God I had no children at twenty-eight, and the list goes on.

But when I'm in the midst of shattered dreams and unfulfilled plans, hindsight is not yet available, nor is it always a comfort. The only thing to rest in is the omnipotence of God. He has a plan—perfect and handcrafted, just for me. *And that includes my beautifully precious and scrumptiously imperfect Lily. God is so sweet to let me cry out, protest, and threaten as He gives me everything I don't want and never asked for but so desperately needed.*

I love you and I'm praying,
Becky

CHAPTER 7 ⦀⦀⦀⦀⦀ Pride

Reasons I'm awesome: 11

Number of people I've judged for not being awesome: 3,672

Faults I work hard to hide: 14

Resolve to fix my faults, live up to my own expectations, and be really good at humility.

ROCK STAR, BROADWAY STYLE

My brother is a Broadway success. For real. For three years he played a role he originated in the laugh-out-loud and fabulous take-Broadway-by-storm *Rock of Ages* (full disclosure: not a family-friendly night out). He's currently one in a cast of five in the brand-new show *Toxic Avenger.* He has performed on *Conan,* the *Today* show, *Regis and Kelly,* and the Tony Awards. He flirted with Liza Minnelli on camera (as a joke, of course, because otherwise that would be super weird), he sings the national anthem for the Giants on occasion, and he gets paid big bucks to be spokesperson Keith Stone, which means his face is on billboards across the country. And in between it all, he makes independent films.

To say I'm crazy proud of my little brother would be an understatement.

But Mitch's rise to a booming career was slow and painful—he paid his dues, for sure. He graduated from Carnegie Mellon ten years ago with hopes of landing a savvy, connected agent, but reality looked more like cattle-call auditions, modest roles that didn't always pay the rent, and ramen noodles. In a 2009 Broadway.com interview, he confessed to singing in the subway for change and one time being so hungry he stole a sandwich from a grocery store.

That one made me cry.

But Mitch stood firm on his career choice, confident in his ability in spite of our family's not-so-subtle suggestions that he move back home to Minnesota. We thought it was loving to be practical, to encourage him to get a steady job and do local theater on the side. After all, making it as an actor is a nearly impossible feat. There are so many talented, driven, beautiful people competing for the same gigs—and simply put, we wanted him to eat. But then came his big break with *Rock of Ages*, where he built his own contact list, gave autographs to his dedicated fans, and began making money hand over fist.

The coolest thing about my brother, though, is his total lack of actor's arrogance. He's confident, for sure, but although he owns the spotlight when he's onstage, he deflects it when he's not. He doesn't love the autograph thing or the extra attention when fans recognize him in public. He's always more interested in what we thought of his fellow cast members than what we thought of him. He's a team player, and somehow the success just hasn't gone to his head. And considering his amazing voice, intense charisma, and perfect comedic timing, I find that astounding.

Quite honestly, I don't identify, because I think I've always erred on the side of arrogance. When we were kids, our family toured around the central Midwest singing in churches during our summer vacations—a Christian version of the Partridge Family. We drove a full-size conversion van, carried our own sound equipment, sold our albums in the church lobby, and brought our dog, Tippy, along. In between gigs, we'd stop at amusement parks and pioneer villages, swim in hotel pools, and have lunch with pastors and their families. And through it all, I was convinced I was the bee's knees. I was a great little singer, and I was certain my dramatic performance was always a crowd pleaser. Meanwhile, Dad didn't even turn Mitch's mic on. He was so little and unpredictable, and didn't even seem to enjoy it—just sang along because that's what our family did on vacation. In other words, while I was obnoxious and puffed up, my Broadway-bound brother flew under the radar.

I've often wondered what it would be like to be Mitch. Not the fame or money as much as the satisfaction of accomplishing something so cool—a confirmation of what I confidently believe about myself already. Ironically, I'm living in a season where everything I thought I knew about myself prior to adopting a four-year-old is proving untrue—because I thought I would be good at this. I thought I would handle the process of adoption with parenting expertise and constant patience because of what our little boy has been through. I thought I'd be able to keep the end game in the forefront when things got tough; I was sure I would maintain perspective. I thought my compassion for orphans and my obedience to God in opening our home would immediately translate into love. I thought I would be doing something that confirmed my good heart—the person I was certain I was. I thought my perfect home would be the perfect fit for Max, and I thought I'd be his perfect mom because being a mom is what I'm good at.

I'm living in a season where everything I thought I knew about myself is proving untrue.

But I was wrong about a lot of things.

FINALLY AND WHAT THE HECK?

After four long years of waiting, we were finally on our way. We flew first class to Thailand because my frequent-flying husband was able to upgrade our seats at the gate, which was amazing. Over the next twenty-six hours, I read two books, watched movies with my feet up, ate at my leisure, caught up on bills and correspondence, chatted with my husband, and slept stretched out in my airplane bed—it couldn't have been better.

Then we landed.

We got to our hotel after midnight and left when the sun came up. According to our caseworker, the plan was to drive to the orphanage, meet our four-year-old, and spend the day getting to know him and his routine before heading back to our hotel alone for a quiet dinner and hotel sex (the latter being our plan, not the caseworker's). The next day we would go back to the orphanage, spend more time getting to know each other, and (if he seemed ready) take our boy back to the hotel. And then forever would commence.

It was a good plan that didn't happen. Instead, we spent an hour at the orphanage (touring the grounds, mostly) before they gave us a kid with the clothes on his back and a bag of chips. I'm not kidding. They handed Max a bag of seaweed-flavored potato chips and sent us on our way. We had no way to communicate with him. No idea what his daily routine was. No idea what foods he liked. No idea how he peed or pooped or slept or bathed. We were suddenly the guardians of one Thai-speaking little boy who, to my great surprise, didn't seem intimidated by his new situation.

Over the next two weeks we struggled and argued and attempted to see the sights while we waited for permission to leave the country. Our other three children were home with my parents, and I missed them so much I couldn't see straight. This new kid wouldn't play with me or any of the toys we'd brought along. He wouldn't look at a book for more than a minute or watch a video without constantly pushing the buttons on the DVD player. He got into suitcases and threw things down the toilet. He laughed when we said no. There was little sleep, lots of chaos, and zero time alone. Seriously. Our bathroom door didn't have a lock, so I couldn't even pee without a miniature stranger watching. He seemed to either be bouncing off the walls of our hotel room or hanging on my husband while we were out, and one thing was clear: he didn't take to me from the start, which was surprisingly A-OK because the connection, feelings, and instincts I was certain I would have never made it to Thailand.

The plane ride home was the perfect precursor to our new life. We had enough miles to upgrade our seats again, but the flight was completely booked, which meant we sat upright in the back of the plane for twenty-six hours. I didn't sleep a wink, though Max sprawled out for more than half the flight, his head on Dallas and his feet on me. I was thankful the wild child slept—no question about that. But I was jet lagged, overwhelmed, and continually kicked, all the while wondering why I felt so unqualified and disconnected from my orphan. I'd been a parent for ten years, I'd risen to the challenge of autism, and I had a giant bleeding heart for adoption. But now this child whose picture I'd stared at for such a long time with raging maternal instinct and love was stressing me out so much I couldn't process how I felt or what I thought or what was true.

We arrived back in the States to my kids, my mom, and my sister and her three boys. They prepared a mini celebration complete with a homemade welcome sign, balloons, food, and an immaculate house—all of which would have thrilled me under normal circumstances but which I was too anxiety ridden to appreciate. Dallas and I put Max to bed early and spent time with our older kids. I felt such nostalgia for our pre-adoption days, I had to hide tears. Around two in the morning I was wide awake, tossing and turning and literally shaking. I felt like I had in high school when I wanted to end it with a boyfriend—when I craved freedom. Only there was no breakup in my future; there was just forever. And in the middle of the night, it was a crushing reality.

Then God told me to get out of bed and open my Bible. With a spiked Capri Sun in one hand (sorry Dad, Nana, my mother-in-law, Pastor James, and Tyndale House Publishers) and my Bible in the other, I prayed and wept and heard from the Lord. He reminded me of His immense, unfailing love. He reminded me that He never leaves us, never forsakes us. He reminded me that I can do all things through Christ who gives me strength, that He had handpicked this little boy for me, that He loved him and would help me love him too. That He would make us a real family, and that I wouldn't always feel the strain and the uncertainty I did in that moment.

And hearing from the Lord has been my saving grace. Literally. Because when I spend time reading my Bible and praying in the morning, I'm a more loving, patient, merciful mommy, and I have peace about the future. When I don't, my selfishness rules the day and I resent my growing family. It's been a painful awakening to my wretched heart, but I get it now—pride comes before a fall.

And I'm still nursing the bruises.

So how in the world did I make it thirty-five years without knowing how selfish I really am? For that matter, why did God throw me in the deep end of the adoption pool, knowing I couldn't swim? And how do I replace the shame I feel about my surprisingly hard heart and weak resolve with the grace God holds outstretched?

How do I find my feet in my weakness?

TRUE GOOD

For the record, Max is an amazing kid. He's brilliant, adorable, charming, and brave. He loves kids, loves music, loves having a family, and loves learning about Jesus. And of course, he didn't stay in Tasmanian devil mode for long; he was just overstimulated by life outside the orphanage, and his brain went nuts. A common reaction, we're told. Granted, Dallas and I are the first parents Max has ever known, which makes him rough around the edges—a frequent saboteur when things are going well and an exacerbator of already challenging days, but we knew that would be the case. The problem really lies with me and my reaction to having my home and life invaded. *My* closed heart. *My* rebellion against the patience and priorities adoption requires. *My* desire for more productive days and quieter nights, and the ease I momentarily experienced with our older children.

But this is my calling. Adoption has been in the cards my entire married life. Shortly after we brought Max home (and while I was still flailing), my brother asked if I regretted my decision to adopt. Huh. I hadn't thought of it that way, and thankfully the answer was no. I have no reservations. No second thoughts. No wishing things were different, and certainly no wanting my precious little boy to go back to the orphanage. I do, however, have a giant weight on my soul because of my inability to do the things I want to do and be the person I want to be—the person I thought I was but really am not.

But I'm in good company.

I don't really understand myself, for I want to do what is right, but I don't do it. Instead, I do what I hate. But if I know that what I am doing is wrong, this shows that I agree that the law is good. So I am not the one doing wrong; it is sin living in me that does it.

> *And I know that nothing good lives in me, that is, in my sinful nature. I want to do what is right, but I can't. I want to do what is good, but I don't. I don't want to do what is wrong, but I do it anyway. But if I do what I don't want to do, I am not really the one doing wrong; it is sin living in me that does it.*
>
> *I have discovered this principle of life—that when I want to do what is right, I inevitably do what is wrong. I love God's law with all my heart. But there is another power within me that is at war with my mind. This power makes me a slave to the sin that is still within me. Oh, what a miserable person I am! Who will free me from this life that is dominated by sin and death? Thank God! The answer is in Jesus Christ our Lord. So you see how it is: In my mind I really want to obey God's law, but because of my sinful nature I am a slave to sin.*
>
> ROMANS 7:15-25, NLT

A miserable person? This was Paul talking. Paul. The one who wrote thirteen of twenty-seven New Testament books and gave us a lion's share of Christian theology; the one who traveled far and wide spreading the Good News about Jesus; the one who was beaten, imprisoned, and martyred for the sake of the gospel he preached; the one important enough to be met by Jesus on the road to Damascus.

So if Paul was frustrated by his recurring sin, I suppose I shouldn't be surprised by my own. I don't know if he struggled with pride specifically; my guess is that after being called out by Jesus while Paul was literally on his way to arrest and kill more Christians, there wasn't much self-congratulating going on. Paul met the God of mercy and second chances, the one who saw beyond the person Paul was at the moment to the person he would become and how he would be powerfully used for the Kingdom. And there's serious encouragement in that. I'm a sinner saved by Jesus, and in spite of my wretchedness, God sees the person I will become—the person I am becoming—by His grace.

In spite of my wretchedness, God sees the person I will become—the person I am becoming—by His grace.

> *I am the true vine, and my Father is the gardener. He cuts off every branch in me that bears no fruit, while every branch that does bear fruit he prunes so that it will be even more fruitful. You are already clean because of the word I have spoken to you. Remain in me, as I also remain in you. No branch can bear fruit by itself; it must remain in the vine. Neither can you bear fruit unless you remain in me.*
>
> *I am the vine; you are the branches. If you remain in me and I in you, you will bear much fruit; apart from me you can do nothing.* JOHN 15:1-5

I've read that passage so many times, but it takes on new meaning after getting my butt kicked by a tiny Asian. I assumed I'd be awesome in our new venture, and I was confused when I wasn't—surprised by my lack of goodness, wisdom, patience, gentleness, and self-control. Surprised, really, by the terrible truth that I didn't like my orphan. But I didn't stand a chance of producing such fruit in the midst of our adoption storm because I was trying to be good apart from the Lord, trying to be the perfect adoptive parent—the perfect Christian—on my own. But as Jesus said, that was never gonna happen.

> *It is because of [God] that you are in Christ Jesus, who has become for us wisdom from God—that is, our righteousness, holiness and redemption. Therefore, as it is written: "Let the one who boasts boast in the Lord."*
> I CORINTHIANS 1:30-31

In an episode of *Friends*, Joey tries to convince Phoebe there's no unselfish good deed—that selfless good deeds simply don't exist. Phoebe is horrified and sets out to prove him wrong. She rakes an old man's yard, but he gives her milk and cookies afterward, which makes her happy, so it doesn't count. She goes to a park and lets a bee sting her, which she brags is a completely selfless act. But Joey points out that her good deed likely killed the bee. She gives $200 to PBS for the joy it brings to children, in spite of her personal issues with Elmo. But her donation helps break the previous year's pledge total, and she's back to getting credit for doing something good.

Joey wasn't wrong, and Phoebe conceded the point. Most of what I do has a payoff of some kind, whether the way it makes me feel or the way it makes me look. Since righteousness, holiness, and redemption come from God—and not from any goodness on my part—I have zero to boast about outside of God's work in and through me.

God is the only good in me. That's it. He's it. If you think you have something to offer other than your allegiance—that God can use you because of your heart, mind, talent, or strength—you don't get it yet. And I caution you: God opposes the proud, and Satan seizes footholds.

Believe me, I know.

> *"God opposes the proud*
> *but shows favor to the humble."*

> *Submit yourselves, then, to God. Resist the devil, and he will*
> *flee from you.* JAMES 4:6-7

During our long wait for Max (and in spite of the fact that I'm not thirteen), I would cry as I listened to Jordin Sparks sing "The

Cure." I'm not sure who it's intended for—it's full of promises to heal a broken heart, to be faithful and patient, and to love like never before. In my mind, it was a song from me to Max. I would be his new mommy, and my love would heal the wounds inflicted by his birth mother when she left him in an apartment in Thailand and never came back.

I couldn't wait to get my hands on him—to love him and fix him.

Of course, it was theologically incorrect to think of myself as Max's healer—only Jesus can heal. But I believed I was the person Jesus would use to heal a broken boy. Little did I know how filthy my righteousness was—is—because God is holy; which is the operative word when it comes to understanding who I am and what my goodness is worth.

> *We are all infected and impure with sin.*
> *When we display our righteous deeds,*
> *they are nothing but filthy rags.*
> *Like autumn leaves, we wither and fall,*
> *and our sins sweep us away like the wind.*
> ISAIAH 64:6, NLT

What a remarkable thing to think you're good and then realize you're not. It sent me spinning. I still find myself trying to be the girl I previously thought I was—if I could just get a good night's sleep and catch up on a few things, I'd calm down and be awesome again. But I can't. I can't. I can fake it (to myself and everyone else) when things are good and life is smooth, but high waves have exposed the truth, and I've got a new song on repeat.

And since it costs too much money to quote, I'll sum up.

"Take My Hand" by Lindsay McCaul and Jason Ingram is

about how God sometimes calls us into the storm—straight toward the wind and waves. While we feel brave at first, circumstances expose our inability to handle the things we thought we could handle—and then fear sets in. But instead of being delivered, we experience God in the midst of the struggle, which I'm finding to be beautiful kind of rescue.

I'm not asking for reasons You hold or the safety of land
I just need You to take my hand

THE ONE WHO LOVES

Rewind to our time in Thailand. We have dear missionary friends who would visit Max when he was still in the orphanage. They brought him books, candy, and pictures of our family, told him about Jesus, and assured him that his new mommy and daddy would come to get him soon. Dallas and I were so grateful that Max was being loved on—we saw it as God's provision and protection for our son while we couldn't be with him. I'm forever indebted, not only because they cared for Max, but also for their help while we were in Bangkok. They showed us around, armed us with maps and sky-train passes when they couldn't be our personal tour guides, translated for us, and were a source of support during a difficult, emotional time.

But by day five, Max still preferred them *and* Dallas over me, and I was sad. From moment one, the entire experience had been nothing I expected. Nothing felt natural or instinctual. Max wasn't connecting to me—the woman he'd seen in pictures for the past year. And what was worse, I didn't feel a connection to him. I excused myself to use the bathroom and cried the moment I was alone, to which God quietly said, "You're going to learn how I love."

I assumed He meant His love is patient and that He faithfully and quietly waits for us to love Him back. Or that He loves us more than we love Him. Or that He loved us first, while we were still stuck and broken. I assumed I was going to learn to love Max patiently and without reciprocation, at least for a while.

But that's not what He meant.

> *Love is patient and kind. Love is not jealous or boastful or proud or rude. It does not demand its own way. It is not irritable, and it keeps no record of being wronged. It does not rejoice about injustice but rejoices whenever the truth wins out. Love never gives up, never loses faith, is always hopeful, and endures through every circumstance.*
>
> *Prophecy and speaking in unknown languages and special knowledge will become useless. But love will last forever! Now our knowledge is partial and incomplete, and even the gift of prophecy reveals only part of the whole picture! But when the time of perfection comes, these partial things will become useless. . . .*
>
> *Three things will last forever—faith, hope, and love—and the greatest of these is love.*
>
> I CORINTHIANS 13:4-10, 13, NLT

I thought God was referring to the way I would love Max, but so far in the process, I'm learning about how God loves *me*. And by His grace, it's spilling over to my son.

What extraordinary mercy for us both.

God is patient when I flail and fail, and when I choose to swim in my selfishness and pride. He's kind. He gives me reprieve when I'm ready to break down—in the form of my friends, my sweet husband, and our parents. He whispers wisdom to help me navigate through the crazy, and He offers conviction to protect the child in my care. He comforts way more than He chastises,

I'm learning about how God loves me. And by His grace, it's spilling over to my son.

even though I usually deserve the latter. He keeps no record of my wrongs, though I've given Him plenty to work with; every day, every repentant minute, I get to start over—His forgiveness has been poured out by the bucketful. He doesn't argue when I'm angry—of course, He doesn't stoop. He lets me wave my fists and tantrum in my heart while He waits for me to yield. Again. And He never boasts. In that little bathroom in Bangkok, He could have said, "I'm amazing. Prepare to be blown away by who I am and who you're not, and how magnificently I love."

But He didn't.

Everything will pass away, and only a few things will remain— the greatest of which is love. And since God *is* love, He's the end-all and be-all, the actual bee's knees, the Alpha and the Omega—take your pick. My recent crash course in the nature of God compared to who I am has been rough because I thought I offered more. I thought my high opinion of my abilities and my good heart was well founded. But as I've begun to see a fuller picture of my sin, God's perfection has come into sharper focus, compelling me to worship like never before, driving me to my knees to glorify the only one who deserves it.

I know my place now, and I'm diggin' the Psalms in a whole new way.

The heavens proclaim the glory of God.
    The skies display his craftsmanship.
Day after day they continue to speak;
    night after night they make him known.
They speak without a sound or word;
    their voice is never heard.

*Yet their message has gone throughout the earth,
    and their words to all the world. . . .*

*How can I know all the sins lurking in my heart?
    Cleanse me from these hidden faults.
Keep your servant from deliberate sins!
    Don't let them control me.
Then I will be free of guilt
    and innocent of great sin.*

*May the words of my mouth
    and the meditation of my heart
be pleasing to you,
    O LORD, my rock and my redeemer.*

PSALM 19:1-4, 12-14, NLT

God used a precious stranger-turned-son to show me who I am, who He is, and how to worship without pride—which is way better, by the way. Praise God I failed so early on and that Max and I didn't lose years to my arrogance and misguided self-confidence. God called me—heck, threw me—into deep water *because* I couldn't swim, because I wouldn't be able to navigate adoption alone.

He forced my dependence because I wouldn't have offered it freely, and I was in desperate need. I don't know how long it'll take to feel the things I want to feel and be the person I want to be, and I don't know when the whole experience will feel wrapped up with a nice, neat bow—we're still in the first-year trenches. But I know God can do all I hope for and more. He'll knit our hearts together. He'll heal Max's wounds. He'll continue to calm my anxiety, and He'll glorify Himself through our obedience in adoption.

God called me—heck, threw me—into deep water because I couldn't swim.

Because I'm finally out of the way.

How do I find my feet in weakness? By remembering to worship God every baby step of the way. And by telling my little boy how magnificently God loves.

CHAPTER 8

Testimony

JUNE 14

People I've shared the gospel with: 17, maybe (Gosh, that's a low number. Hopefully I'm forgetting a few.)

Awkward moments I've experienced for Jesus: 9

Converts from my gospel pitch: 1

Friends with better testimonies than me: 5

Resolve to perfect my gospel presentation and win people for Jesus. And to make Jesus look cool by being a really good Christian and by keeping it all together.

THE REDHEAD WHO RULES

I have a really cool friend I met in LA when I was pregnant with my third kiddo. I was throwing up all day, every day, and taking care of the two children I already had—and my mom was two thousand miles away. A friend from Tennessee (also very cool) called a local church for help. She asked if someone in their women's ministry could reach out to me with meals or babysitting or whatever I needed. She gave them my number, and a few days later I got a call from a girl named Regan, who said, "Hi. I go to church in Santa Monica, and I hear you're pregnant with your third kid. You must be exhausted. I'm bringing you a meal."

Who does that? Well, Regan does.

Normally I would've graciously declined. I'm a perfectionist who doesn't receive help willingly. I don't like to impose, and I certainly don't want people to think I'm struggling—that would defeat the purpose of appearing to be perfect. But I was constantly sick, with a toddler bouncing off the walls and a nine-month-old whining at my feet, and a prepared meal sounded like a gift from the Lord. Though as it turned out, the gifter was the gift.

Regan showed up at my door with lasagna, garlic bread, salad, and her newborn baby—which means she pushed out a kid and then signed up to make dinner for a stranger. I was amazed by her selflessness. Not only that, but she was hilarious and cool and clearly passionate about Jesus. When my morning sickness passed a few weeks later, she and her husband invited Dallas and me over for dinner.

The rest is friendship history.

And after almost a decade, I can easily say that the thing I love most about Regan is her transparency and willingness to share her unique testimony—because not everyone in her shoes would. She's a rock star for Jesus, totally committed and surrendered to the truth about who she is, who God is, and the redemptive work He has done in her life. She shares her story in spite of her instinct to protect herself; she puts the cringe aside when she's asked to speak to a large group of women about her past (*and* when her friend wants to put it in a book). She wants her prodigal story to glorify God and to inspire and compel people to run to Him. She's a heavyweight in the testimony department. She's been there. Done that. And as a girl who has no real drama in her story, I'm envious of Regan's ability to captivate listeners and point them to Jesus—her rescuer—in a way that makes them think twice about what the world offers or what Christians don't understand or how Jesus is the King of mercy who pursues us to the depths.

And it goes something like this.

A LAND FAR AWAY

Sweet Regan was a Christian when she was in high school. She knew the truth about Jesus and had the assurance of salvation, but during her junior year she came to a fork in the road, and everything changed. She developed a surprising attraction to a smart, interesting, knowledgeable female teacher. When she shared her feelings, the woman assured her that nothing would happen—that Regan was "safe" with her. But a few months later, they began a physical relationship that lasted for the next four years.

She calls them the darkest of her life.

At a recent women's conference, she explained:

My life was full of lies and isolation, the two of us living in our own little world. We lived together when I moved to New York for college, and there I hid with her. During that time, I made desperate attempts to reclaim my faith, but God— because He is a rightly jealous God—would not bend to my will. It wasn't like He was gone; He just let me leave. I went to church and felt nothing. I read the Bible a few times and felt nothing. I prayed and heard only silence in response. But God's stillness never bothered me enough to give up my relationship. Because as some of you know, relationships can act as a God-substitute for a long, long time.

The two of them split after Regan's college graduation because Regan was unwilling to tell her family about the relationship. The affair had, after all, started when she was just a kid in school. Her parents would likely say their minor daughter had been taken advantage of and abused by her teacher (which is actually what happened, but I digress).

Now single and committed to the gay lifestyle, Regan began thinking about how she would come out to her family. But at her mom's fiftieth birthday bash, she was seated next to a guy who was funny, smart, and chatty, and she found herself completely attracted to him, which shot a few holes in her "I'm a lesbian" theory.

In the weeks that followed, the two exchanged e-mails, and she worked up the courage to tell him she was gay. She expected his response to be disappointment or shock, but instead he just said, "Oh . . . okay." She asked if he thought it was possible for a Christian to be gay, and he responded in the most graceful way possible: he told her to read her Bible and ask God that question.

She writes:

> *Of course, the Bible speaks pretty clearly on the subject, and reading it for myself finally took me to the Cross. Because in my attempts to get around the clear verses that speak against the sin of homosexuality, I kept feeling a pull from God. Not a harsh voice, but a call to come home.*
>
> *So I came home, literally and spiritually. I woke up on the first morning of the twenty-first century and knew I needed to come out to my parents. Not in the way I thought I would come out a few years prior, but like the Prodigal Son. It was pretty much the power of God that led me down the hall to my parents' room that morning. It was God who opened my mouth, God who fashioned my very first testimony, and God who healed us all.*

Regan later married a wonderful man she describes as her best friend and the love of her life. Together they have two precious boys. She says that when she looks at their little faces, she often hears God say, "See them, Regan? This is what I had waiting for you. I'm glad you came home." She's blessed and fulfilled, though she doesn't claim her life is perfect. She's honest about the fact that she hasn't been delivered from her attraction to women; she's living in what she calls "remission," and she plans on doing so for the rest of her life.

She guards against temptation and lives each day in God's forgiveness and power. She shares her story in spite of potential repercussions that Christians might judge her and non-Christians might despise her for calling the gay lifestyle sin. She tells people about the saving grace of Jesus and how being in a close relationship with God is the single greatest thing in her life. And she oozes His love because she knows it well. She's my amazing, truth-telling, forgiving, and inspiring friend, and I'm so proud of her courage.

And while I certainly don't envy the pain she's endured, I do wish my testimony were remotely as interesting or compelling. My story from the beginning to the present goes like this: I came to Jesus when I was five or thereabout, and I've been fairly well behaved ever since. I went to a Christian college and majored in Bible. I got married to a great Christian guy at the age of twenty-one—both of us were virgins. I have four kids, and they go to a Christian school run by the church where my husband recently started working. We've helped plant a church, taught Bible studies, and hosted small groups.

Blah-dee-blah-blah-puke.

So boring, right? I'm brown rice and the color gray in the world of testimonies, and yet I admit my story falls in line with the facade I perpetuate—that I have it all together, which is the mantra of any good perfectionist. For a long time now I've believed my own press—that if I act right, look right, and speak right, people will wonder how I do it and be drawn to Jesus. I'm His ambassador, after all; my husband and I are surrendered to Christ, which equals being good and happy and steady and clean and healthy and kind, thereby making the Jesus road look good.

And it's a load of crap because I'm learning the hard way that

I've lived out some horrifyingly bad theology that brings very few people to Jesus—but more of those sad details in a minute.

So what's a testimony *supposed* to be for those of us without a cool story? Are testimonies primarily our come-to-Jesus moments, or is there more to be told? The most powerful stories seem to be the ones where people give their lives to Jesus and turn everything around, 180 degrees, with spiritual fruit that grows at a rapid rate. But the start of my journey is boring, and now I'm running a-perfectionist-muck.

> *I'm learning the hard way that I've lived out some horrifyingly bad theology that brings very few people to Jesus.*

I love Jesus, and I love people. I'm passionate and sincere about wanting to see them come to Him. I weep when I see altar calls because there's nothing more beautiful than watching people give their lives to God. But I'm personally not reaping much of a spiritual harvest. So putting aside all my misguided efforts to say and do and be, what *really* draws people to Jesus?

As my stats make plain, heck if I know.

DELTA GAMMA GIRL

Regan and I used to share a fabulous babysitter. She was mine first—I passed her name along when Regan needed someone new. And even though Gina had been coming to my house for a couple of years already, it was Regan who suggested we ask our sorority sitter to do a Bible study with us.

Hmm, that hadn't occurred to me. Don't get me wrong—I'd been praying for Gina for a long time, and I tried in earnest to let Jesus shine. I cared about her deeply, though I hadn't put gospel words to my actions. I guess I was waiting for the right moment, and I wanted to build our friendship first—I needed to earn the right to share, or at least that's what I read in a book one time.

Quite honestly, the idea of suggesting a Bible study scared me. Regan and I were moms, for grief's sake, and Gina was a beautiful, popular college girl. Why on earth would she want to? But as it turned out, she *was* interested, and so were the six other Delta Gamma girls she invited. Every Monday night we had the privilege of watching

> *Jesus doesn't need us to be cool—just willing.*

Gina soak up Scripture like a sponge and eventually surrender her life to Jesus. And I, of course, was convicted by the fact that while I'd been waiting for the right moment to present the gospel in the coolest way possible, Regan threw caution to the wind. She knew Jesus didn't need us to be cool—just willing—and she obeyed when He convicted her to speak up.

Makes me think of Paul and his hard-coreness.

Obviously, I'm not trying to win the approval of people, but of God. If pleasing people were my goal, I would not be Christ's servant.

> *Dear brothers and sisters, I want you to understand that the gospel message I preach is not based on mere human reasoning. I received my message from no human source, and no one taught me. Instead, I received it by direct revelation from Jesus Christ.* GALATIANS 1:10-12, NLT

Evangelism 101. We're supposed to share Jesus with boldness and let the chips fall where they may because we're seeking God's approval, not people's. And our message comes direct from the all-powerful Creator and King, which should drive out fear. And any appearance of having it all together is a lie anyway, since I mess up and burn out on a regular basis.

Unfortunately, my perfectionism is the enemy of my duty to share because it fools me into believing that when I'm super cool and witty, or when I look great and fashion-forward, or when I'm intelligent enough to remember all the "evidence that demands a verdict," then and only then will I change someone's mind about Jesus. When my babysitter turned into a Jesus freak, I understood pretty quickly that it's not about me and that God alone reveals truth to people—even the ones we love the most.

Then again, the past year of silence between me and my little brother indicates I still have a lot to learn.

> *Do you think I have come to bring peace to the earth? No, I have come to divide people against each other! From now on families will be split apart, three in favor of me, and two against—or two in favor and three against.*
>
> *"Father will be divided against son*
> *   and son against father;*
> *mother against daughter*
> *   and daughter against mother;*
> *and mother-in-law against daughter-in-law*
> *   and daughter-in-law against mother-in-law."*
> LUKE 12:51-53, NLT

Or sister against brother.

TIES THAT BIND

Ever since Mitch told me he didn't believe in Jesus, that passage from Luke has haunted me. So in order to avoid any possible rift between us, I've tried to say and do all the right things to combat the way Mitch sees Christianity and, of course, the way he sees me. But walking on eggshells didn't prevent the fallout waiting to happen, because in spite of my effort to build our relationship, present Jesus in a more likable way, and avoid overdoing the Christian-speak, Mitch stopped talking to me last winter. He'd been distancing himself from our family for a few months already—no blowup to speak of; he just wasn't keeping in touch. But then he e-mailed me a short film he'd made that portrayed Jesus as an unfeeling, entitled, trust-fund baby; God as the ruthless, merciless dictator; and Satan as the hardworking victim of God's reckless condemnation who sees the good in people God has banished to hell.

And it triggered something deep in my soul. I wanted to say, "What the heck? I'm *with* Jesus! If you knew me or respected me at all, you wouldn't have sent this!" Though, of course, I didn't use those words or end my sentences with exclamation points. Surprising gut reaction, considering Mitch already knew where I stood, but in that moment I realized I'd been tempering that part of my life around my beloved little brother for fear it would push him away. Don't get me wrong—Mitch knows I'm a committed Christian, and he'll be surprised to hear I tempered anything. Ever. But I always tried to be careful with my words because I didn't want him to run further away—and because I thought God could use a little help in the reputation department. It took that video to push me off the fence.

After I shared my piece, Mitch wouldn't return my calls or texts. I was heartbroken, but also ticked. I responded nicely—my words had been carefully and prayerfully chosen, and it was the first time in a long time I'd expressed any frustration at all. I had worked so hard to keep this sort of thing from happening. I thought I'd been cool enough to secure his favor and faithful enough to be honest. But being awesome (at least in my own mind, but whatever, I'm making a point) didn't prevent our estrangement, and it certainly didn't make my brother change his mind about Jesus. It just postponed what may have been inevitable. Because the gospel divides—that we're promised. It doesn't give us a license to be harsh, or to speak truth apart from love *or* apart from the leading of the Holy Spirit. But the gospel offends those who don't believe it, and no amount of presentation or pandering can mask what they want no part of.

Truthfully, I really wonder if my entire relationship with my brother would have been different (i.e., better) if I'd been more authentic along the way, more honest about my weaknesses and wonderings—if I had left behind the perfectionist persona a long time ago. I wonder how Mitch would have responded if he'd known how much I really *do* struggle with pride and insecurity, depending on the day. Or if I'd shared how lonely LA could be, how hard being a mom is, how long and daunting the next fifteen years of parenting feels, and how I sometimes question God and the things He allows. I wanted my walk with Christ to look happy and easy and settled, and more attractive than the path Mitch was on. But my strategy clearly didn't have the effect I was going for, and I wish I could go back and implement the things I'm learning now. Not just for Mitch's sake, but also for my own. Because transparency is the necessary starting place for testimony, not to mention relationship—be it our first Jesus moment or all the times we experience Him on the road.

> *Transparency is the necessary starting place for testimony, not to mention relationship.*

Most important, I think I forgot that God alone saves. I mean, I know that, but I clearly didn't *know* that. I felt such pressure to pull my brother back into the fold. I'm the big sister, and as far back as I can remember, I've wanted to protect him. When we were five and three, I tried to convince him to ask Jesus into his heart in case a lion ate him at the zoo. On vacation, I wouldn't let him stand too close to the edge of the Grand Canyon, and if anyone had messed with him when we were in high school, I would've done some serious damage (no doubt, *he* would've preferred getting beat up to being rescued by his big sister).

But only the Holy Spirit reveals truth to lost hearts. Even on my best day, or with an amazing testimony like Regan's, or under the duress of a hungry lion, I can't win somebody for Jesus. The past year of silence was bound to come sooner or later, I think, because Mitch needed the space—and because God wanted to teach me I truly can't drag my brother into heaven.

But He can.

God is our refuge and strength,
*   an ever-present help in trouble.*
Therefore we will not fear, though the earth give way
*   and the mountains fall into the heart of the sea,*
though its waters roar and foam
*   and the mountains quake with their surging.*

There is a river whose streams make glad the city of God,
*   the holy place where the Most High dwells.*
God is within her, she will not fall;
*   God will help her at break of day.*
Nations are in uproar, kingdoms fall;
*   he lifts his voice, the earth melts.*

The LORD Almighty is with us;
*   the God of Jacob is our fortress.*

Come and see what the LORD has done,
*   the desolations he has brought on the earth.*
He makes wars cease
*   to the ends of the earth.*

> *He breaks the bow and shatters the spear;*
> *he burns the shields with fire.*
> *He says, "Be still, and know that I am God;*
> *I will be exalted among the nations,*
> *I will be exalted in the earth."*
>
> *The LORD Almighty is with us;*
> *the God of Jacob is our fortress.*
> PSALM 46

In my search for comforting verses on God's power to save, I found this psalm. It's not as conventional as other passages, and I'm mulling it—wrestling, really. Because on the one hand, it explains why I should have total confidence in God's ability to save—He can do the impossible. He can move mountains and save souls. Nothing happens that He doesn't allow, and nothing and no one can resist His commands. I'm comforted by it, fired up, and excited to see what my great and powerful God is going to do in my brother's life and heart. But on the other hand, from a nonbeliever's point of view, I wonder if it makes God seem arrogant, callous, brutal, or unfeeling. The desolation He brings to His enemies, the fire and pain He inflicts on the earth, and the demand that He be exalted trigger my instinct to censor for the sake of God's reputation (the grace, love, and mercy stuff seems to play so much better). Anything that can be construed as yucky or harsh makes me feel defensive, and I avoid it. I censor.

So my problem with sharing my testimony—or the gospel, for that matter—is threefold. I don't have an interesting story to back up my claims, I feel the need to make Christianity look good by living a "perfect" life, and I feel it's my duty to soften God's reputation—all of which are obvious obstacles to reaching people for Jesus because they're ridiculously self-focused. Seeing it all on paper makes me cringe, since it certainly doesn't line up with what I know to be true—God alone saves, and people aren't drawn to perfect people anyway; we're drawn to imperfect people we can identify with, people who have found answers to the things that ail.

So how do I drop my perfectionist approach to being Christ's ambassador? And what's the right way to be authentic? Ha—very apropos . . . the *right* way. Let me try again. How do I combat my sinful, self-focused, insecure tendencies when it comes to sharing the gospel? How do I tell the truth and let the chips fall?

Practice, practice, practice.

> *People aren't drawn to perfect people; we're drawn to imperfect people we can identify with, people who have found answers to the things that ail.*

SQUASHED

Let's start with today. Today I've been yelling at my kids. Dallas is out of town and school is out, and the kids are constantly arguing or telling me they're bored. I'm exhausted, and I'm stressed about making progress on my book, and the house is a mess—and I'm yelling at my kids. I've been convicted numerous times and have apologized to the kids a few of those times, but my impatience and selfishness have remained, ready to boil over on the next miniature person to cross me. Then, about thirty minutes ago, I locked myself in the bathroom and spent a moment with God. I read this verse because that's the page I opened my Bible to. And slowly the angry fog is lifting.

> *This is the message we heard from Jesus and now declare to you: God is light, and there is no darkness in him at all. So we are lying if we say we have fellowship with God but go on living in spiritual darkness; we are not practicing the truth. But if we are living in the light, as God is in the light, then*

we have fellowship with each other, and the blood of Jesus,
his Son, cleanses us from all sin.

If we claim we have no sin, we are only fooling ourselves
and not living in the truth. But if we confess our sins to him,
he is faithful and just to forgive us our sins and to cleanse us
from all wickedness.   1 JOHN 1:5-9, NLT

That's the foundation for all testimony. All the things I hate about myself—my quick trigger, my buried anger, my defensiveness, my insecurity, my pride, my judgmental heart, and my selfishness—are forgiven and poured out when I go to Jesus and confess. And in place of my brokenness is spiritual fruit, which I had no chance of producing or sustaining on my own. Patience, joy, kindness, selflessness—those are the qualities I possess only when I spend time with the Lord. The good in me is Jesus; the bad in me is me.

> *The good in me is Jesus; the bad in me is me.*

So the solution to my wretched self is easy:

[Jesus] must become greater and greater, and I must become
less and less.   JOHN 3:30, NLT

And the solution to wanting a more compelling testimony—or just a more honest one—is easy too: be authentic.

For years I heard, "You're adopting? Oh, you're such a good person!" Now that we have our little boy, I hear it even more. I pretty much always knew it wasn't true—God is love and God helps us love and all that jazz. I used to smile and say thanks, not wanting to give an awkward response like, "No . . . God is love, and God helps us love," etc. But now that we've been through the adoption, and I've struggled so significantly throughout the entire process, I can't accept the compliment. I'm physically incapable of saying, "Thank you"—it would feel utterly false. I usually preface my response with, "Um, this is going to sound socially awkward, but no—I'm not a good person. I'm wretched. *Wretch-ed.* God makes me kind. God makes me patient. God loves orphans, and by His grace, He's making me love mine."

I can't take the credit. I can't.

I'm a sinner in desperate need of the saving and sustaining power of Jesus—the one who compelled me to love a little boy He loved first. The one who steadies me, convicts me, restores me, and pours out wisdom for the unique obstacles Dal and I now face. And all that on a daily basis. Hang with me for an afternoon, and you're going to see a sinful woman who is being transformed by gospel power.

That's my testimony.

If we are living in the light, as God is in the light, then we have fellowship with each other, and the blood of Jesus, his Son, cleanses us from all sin. I JOHN 1:7, NLT

I'm going to live in the light. I'm going to be honest about my struggles so I can be honest about how God is the only good in me. I'm going to boast in my weakness so that God's strength will be revealed in it. I want God to get the glory when I'm *not* wretched, because He's the author of righteousness. And I want to have true fellowship with other people—relationship that is born of transparency and truth.

On that note, I'm praising God for my recently restored relationship with my brother, a relationship I hope to be more authentic in. I want him and anyone else who may be watching to see God's redemption story playing out on the pages of my life. And I want that story to have one aim, one focus. God loves me, God saved me, and God is redeeming me, because that's what He does. It's what every testimony from the beginning of time has been made of: "I was . . . , but God . . . , and now . . ."

I was a controlling, insecure, selfish perfectionist who held myself and everyone else to a ridiculous and painfully high standard. But God has humbled me—squashed me—and shown me who I really am: a sinner in desperate need of forgiveness and transformation. And now He's making me more like Jesus—humble and patient, forgiving and gracious, first and foremost to a precious little boy who was handpicked for our family.

I was, but God, and now.

DANCING TILL WE DROP

Yesterday Regan and I had the privilege of reading some passages of Scripture at Gina's wedding. And at the reception we danced our butts off with our husbands and Regan's two little boys—the ring bearers in the ceremony, who tore it up on the dance floor. Apparently they've taken hip-hop classes, and at three feet tall, they're as smoooov as anyone I've seen.

But aside from being a much-needed night out and a total blast with friends I adore, the reception was also a fabulous picture of the way we're redeemed. Because God doesn't pull us from the muck and mire to sit us on the sidelines; He wants us to *dance*. To experience life to the fullest. He wants Regan to swing her hips with her amazing husband and to laugh with friends who know her fully and wholly and who love her, scars and struggles and all. He wants us to walk the Jesus road in truth so we're not alone with our junk and so we don't struggle in the dark, where everything gets bigger and scarier and more powerful.

He wants us to extend our hands to each other when we fall down. He wants us to keep each other accountable because He knows sin hurts the people He loves. But most of all, He wants us to know Him, and He wants the people watching His children to be drawn to Him—the author and perfecter of our faith. He wants glory for the gift of life He offers freely and for the spiritual fruit He produces in us—the love, joy, peace, patience, kindness, goodness, faithfulness, gentleness, and self-control we couldn't possibly produce on our own (Galatians 5:22-23). And He wants us to remember. To know with great clarity our own stories so we don't wander or lose heart or give apathy a foothold.

He wants us to know our testimonies.

And He wants us to know He's not done writing them.

CHAPTER 9 ⫶⫶⫶⫶⫶ Obedience

People I admire for being really good: 11

Things I do regularly that are bad: 3

Ways I try to earn back my good standing with Jesus: 4

Resolve to stop messing up and be more self-controlled with my money and my tongue; to be who God wants and go where He wants and do what He wants; to not be a hypocrite, to be awesome even when no one's looking, and to make God happy by being good.

SOUL SISTER

Ashley Davidson is one of my favorite people on earth and has been for a long time. She's hardworking, thoughtful, hilariously sarcastic, nurturing, pop-culturally savvy, and downright fun. We met when we worked at a Christian bookstore in Louisville, Kentucky, more than thirteen years ago—both newly married and without children so we had plenty of time to bond, which happened almost instantly. We shopped together, ate together, went away for girls' weekends, laughed our way through the workday, and forced our husbands to be friends, too—which came easily.

The two quickly formed their own relationship, along with an accountability group that has become part of church lore. But that's a different story. Maybe a different book.

Over the years I've watched Ashley grow as an obedient, committed Christian who takes her walk with God seriously. Even when we were working with older, wiser women, it was Ashley who pointed out all the backbiting and gossiping we girls fall into, and she led the way in repentance and self-control. Her husband, Matt, was a youth pastor and then a worship pastor, which put her in the front pew—literally and figuratively—and she has served the church faithfully her entire married life, opening her home, traveling with youth groups, and leading Bible studies. She's good at doing the right thing. Bottom line, she's good at loving the people in her life. She's humble enough to know she still has a long way to go, and she's gracious to those of us who don't always know the same about ourselves.

I'm blessed to know her.

When Dallas and I decided to move to LA in 2000, I was sad to say good-bye to my friend, especially since both of us were pregnant with our first babies—both boys. But we remained close in spite of the distance, so four years later when she told me she was moving to California too, I was ecstatic . . . though Ashley wasn't. She grew up in Louisville and has always been super close to her family. The thought of leaving them and everyone else she'd known her entire life was hard. But there was no denying it was God's plan, because He'd told her so straight-up in Starbucks.

She and Matt were with another couple when she heard that unmistakable still, small voice telling her that their ministry was moving to the Golden State. Ugh. She tried to ignore it and carried on in conversation as if nothing had happened. She wrestled with the news for the next few days before surrendering and bringing Matt up to speed. They had lots of questions about what God's announcement over coffee meant, but two weeks later, a job offer arrived from the very *un*glamorous Moorpark, California—a desert city about an hour and a half outside of LA. And within a matter of months, their little family obediently uprooted and headed west.

Unfortunately, Ashley's new stomping ground was pretty far from where I lived, which meant lots of traveling and less time together than we would have liked. We made trips to each other's houses a couple of times a month, but the distance, combined with LA traffic and small children in preschool, made it hard. *And* Moorpark itself was a bummer because it's uncomfortably hot and the landscape is permanently yellow—a sad departure from the lush, changing seasons of the Bluegrass State. *And* the cost of living was California-crazy high, so all the Davidsons could afford was a puke-brown stucco rental with sea foam green carpet, which didn't exactly jibe with Ashley's fab decorating taste. *And* a mean man lived next door. He complained every time the youth group barbecued in the backyard. *And* in order to afford it all, they had to ask friends and acquaintances for financial contributions to supplement Matt's salary, which was a scary and humbling endeavor.

But in spite of all the things she didn't like about their new circumstances, Ashley held fast to what she knew: this was God's plan, and she really was surrendered to it. Her job was to trust and serve Him no matter what—or where. She had no doubt they were doing what the Lord wanted them to and that He'd take care of them, financially, emotionally, and otherwise. Which, of course, He did. He proved himself faithful and good, and Ashley and her family experienced the Lord's sufficiency in the desert.

And I'm beginning to think it was practice for what was coming eight short years later.

A TIME TO WEEP

Matt and Ashley eventually made it back to their hometown of Louisville, where Matt landed his dream job as the worship pastor at Southeast Christian Church, Oldham Campus—a plant of the megachurch they grew up in. They were extremely happy to be home among family and friends, especially since their household continued to grow. Their three kiddos were eleven, five, and two, and their extended family kept popping out more cousins. It was a peaceful, sweet time of communion with the ones they loved most and a respite from the ministry challenges of previous years.

Then, a little over a month ago, tragedy struck.

The Davidson family was planning to spend the weekend at our house for a long-overdue visit, and we were counting down the days. But the Tuesday before, I got a text from Ash saying Matt had been in an accident. He was stable but had a broken hip. Apparently he'd been driving home from work and was hit head-on by a guy trying to avoid a rabbit on the road. We were thankful he was okay, but sad we weren't going to see them. Ashley and I stayed in touch throughout the week and prayed over the surgery needed to repair the broken bones. The procedure went well, and the prognosis was good. Matt was in good spirits, frequently praying for his visitors and the nursing staff—which is *so* Matt. He represented Jesus the way he always did, caring for and loving the people in his path. Even from a hospital bed.

I texted Ashley on Saturday morning to check in. I wanted to know how Matt was doing and if our care package had arrived. The message I got back is burned in my brain—"Oh, AJ, he went to be with Jesus at 9:27." I couldn't breathe. I stared at my phone, thinking it had to be a bad joke, only that wasn't something Ashley would do. It just didn't make sense; he was supposed to be released on Monday to go home and start rehab. I ran to my computer to check the Facebook updates of our Kentucky friends and immediately found what I was looking for. Matt had suffered a pulmonary embolism—a massive blood clot that had traveled to his lungs. It was fast moving and unsurvivable.

And at thirty-six, he was gone.

I went upstairs to tell Dallas what had happened but started hyperventilating and couldn't get it out. In a blink, my treasured friend was a widow, her children fatherless. It's an impossible thing to process. I had been grieving our lost weekend, knowing it would be a long time before our schedules lined up again—how ridiculous that seemed now.

It has been five weeks since that morning, and we're still trying to acclimate, missing Matt terribly and working hard to trust the Lord. And Ash is in a new kind of desert, only this time she's there as a single mom, and it stretches as far as the eye can see.

So the question is obvious and impossible to answer: Why? Matt and Ashley served God faithfully together. They encouraged each other to grow and kept each other accountable. They tried to be an example of love and of Christ's mercy in their neighborhood, at their kids' schools, and in church. Their life's pursuit was to glorify the Lord. But now Ashley is afraid her children will wander from the faith because their dad, who followed and obeyed Jesus, was taken too soon. She's afraid her little people might not be satisfied by the answers to impossible questions.

And I'm not that different. I mean, I'm a big girl now, and I'd like to think I've matured in the faith enough not to be derailed when bad things happen to good people. Even when they're *my* people. But trials and tragedy expose what remains at my core— a wrong view of what obedience can earn and, conversely, what disobedience can lose. Clearly, Matt's good behavior didn't earn him good things or a long life any more than they earned his way into heaven. And, of course, any bad behavior didn't remove God's favor, because His grace is poured out freely through Jesus Christ.

Thing is, Matt had an extraordinary grasp of that grace, and it colored every interaction he had with the people who crossed his path. I would be horrified by some behavior at church or some teenage girl's uber-short skirt, and I'd be all, "Oh my gosh, I can't believe this or that." But Matt always said something like, "Well, at least she came to church" or "I remember when I used to struggle with that too"—always some merciful response that put me to shame. I want to learn from Matt even now, in his death, which means that instead of asking why my friend had to die so young, I should be asking why he lived to obey. Of course, I already know the answer: Matt saw obedience as a way to honor the God who saved him, not as a way to earn His love. And certainly not as a measuring stick to judge others.

> *Grace is a big hill to climb for a perfectionist like me.*

But grace is a big hill to climb for a perfectionist like me.

And then there's Maya.

PINT-SIZE PERFECTIONIST

I'm raising a very spunky nine-year-old who is as big a joy as she is a challenge. She's outgoing and brave, competitive, focused, and extraordinarily people-smart. She reads faces and doesn't miss a beat. She knows what I'm thinking before I say it, and she's a sponge—a super-teachable people pleaser, which makes her an amazing athlete and student, and a quintessential overachiever.

And so, in spite of her giftedness, I worry for Maya because not only does she experience a lot of self-imposed pressure (especially for someone so young), but she also often accomplishes her goals for the wrong reasons. She wants people to like her. She's zealous for rules. She trashes a picture she spent an hour coloring because she made one mistake. She adjusts quickly to instruction because she's got to get it "right" and be impressive.

In a lot of ways, she's just like me. Sigh. So sorry, kid.

When I see the burden to do everything right sitting squarely on her little shoulders, I'm sad for her. It grieves me because as her mom, I know the pressure is unnecessary—she's loved and accepted already, without condition. I wish she were motivated to obey in school because she loves to gain knowledge and honor her teacher, or to strive in athletics because she adores the intricacies of the game, or to comply at home because she trusts her dad and me and wants to show her family love. I mean, there's some of that, but it lives alongside the yoke of slavery I've experienced for so long—the drive to obey *so that*.

I obey *so that* people will like me. I obey *so that* people will think I'm awesome and have it all together. I obey *so that* I don't get in trouble or cause a scene, thereby drawing attention to the fact that I didn't obey. Grief—I obey *so that* I can obey. It has become its own end—obedience for the sake of obedience—which, by the way, is a motive with no staying power, no gratification, and no attraction for nonbelievers.

And it doesn't please the Lord.

> *"What makes you think I want all your sacrifices?"*
>   *says the LORD.*
> *"I am sick of your burnt offerings of rams*
>   *and the fat of fattened cattle.*
> *I get no pleasure from the blood*
>   *of bulls and lambs and goats."*
> ISAIAH 1:11, NLT

Why would God say He didn't want the sacrifices He'd previously commanded the Israelites to bring? In context, the answer is clear: because their sacrifices were no longer being given out of the overflow of their love for God or as an outward demonstration of their commitment to following Him. Instead, their lives were full of unrepentant sin and idol worship. They gave sacrifices because they were supposed to; it was part of their tradition and culture. But God wasn't fooled by their actions because He saw their hearts.

And hearts are God's primary order of business. When Jesus was preaching the Sermon on the Mount—the sermon detailing the attributes we're supposed to strive for—He emphasized that God judges the heart and that being obedient in action only simply isn't enough.

Matthew 5 says:

> *You have heard that our ancestors were told, "You must not murder."* . . . *But I say, if you are even angry with someone, you are subject to judgment!*
>
> *You have heard the commandment that says, "You must not commit adultery." But I say, anyone who even looks at a woman with lust has already committed adultery with her in his heart.*
>
> *You have heard the law that says, "Love your neighbor" and hate your enemy. But I say, love your enemies! Pray for those who persecute you!*
> VERSES 21-22, 27-28, 43-44, NLT

And on it goes, the entire sermon dealing with matters of the heart. As I think about it, I realize how often I obey the letter of the law for the wrong reasons—how often I do the right thing with the wrong attitude or misguided motive.

And sadly, that's how it's been for a long time.

When I was exactly Maya's age, I happened upon a group of kids plotting to be horribly mean to a girl in our class. I had just gotten hot lunch and was carrying my tray toward the tables where we usually sat, when my classmates gestured for me to quickly sit down in the last available seat. I did, though I was confused by all the urgency and whispering. Seconds later I realized they had conspired to make Colleen sit by herself. I don't remember exactly what they said to her as she approached, but it was awful. She sat down at the other table and started to cry while they jeered and laughed.

I was horrified. It was so wrong, and the Holy Spirit stirred in my little soul, though I sat frozen, weighing my options. Then I remembered Colleen was a bit of a teacher's pet, and I certainly didn't want Mrs. S. to think I had any part in the cruel plan.

My self-preservation tipped the scale.

I stood up, tray in hand, and sat in the seat next to Colleen. The meanness of the crowd transferred to me, but it didn't last long—I think they were surprised anyone had the guts to defect, and they just went back to eating. I don't remember either of us saying a word, but Colleen eventually stopped crying and I stayed with her for the rest of lunch and recess. I didn't have a choice, really; in a flash, it was us against them. Even my best friend and blood buddy (such a weird and gross pre–AIDS era ritual) symbolically washed her hands, which included her previously pricked finger, and stormed away.

And all that to say, now that I'm a mom, I'm so, so, so glad I sat next to that precious girl—so thankful she didn't have to endure the torture alone. I can't stand bullying, and I cringe at the thought of it happening to one of my own. I'm glad God used me to help stop Colleen's tears, but I wish I'd done it for the right reasons. I wish I hadn't hesitated when Christ's compassion was convicting my heart. I wish my good standing with my teacher hadn't been more important to me than what pleased the Lord. I wish I had obeyed because I'm unconditionally loved by God and I couldn't ignore something that hurt His heart. There were lots of good reasons to sit by Colleen that day, but impressing my teacher wasn't one of them. Her approval was a pathetic consolation prize compared to how proud God might've otherwise been.

MY SPIRITUAL B

In spite of my tendency to obey for all the wrong reasons, God in His sovereignty and abundant grace still draws near to self-centered people like me, just as He did with Israel. Even after rescuing them from slavery in Egypt, leading and feeding them through the desert, delivering them in battle and giving them the Promised Land, their hearts wandered. He warned them. He tried to wake them up to their sin by sending prophets like Isaiah and Jeremiah, but the people wouldn't listen, and discipline became necessary to bring them back to Him. And yet here's what God said was going to happen to the unfaithful people He would not turn His back on:

> *God in His sovereignty and abundant grace still draws near to self-centered people like me.*

> *"In that day," says the LORD, "I will be the God of all the families of Israel, and they will be my people. This is what the LORD says:*
>
> *"Those who survive the coming destruction*
> *will find blessings even in the barren land,*
> *for I will give rest to the people of Israel."*
>
> *Long ago the LORD said to Israel:*
> *"I have loved you, my people, with an everlasting love.*
> *With unfailing love I have drawn you to myself.*
> *I will rebuild you, my virgin Israel.*
> *You will again be happy*

and dance merrily with your tambourines.
Again you will plant your vineyards on the mountains of Samaria
and eat from your own gardens there."
JEREMIAH 31:1-5, NLT

I've always been fascinated by God's faithfulness to Israel, although only in recent years have I started to truly identify with their idiocy (I was always an idiot; I just recently became aware of it). I *am* Israel, my heart's pendulum frequently swaying between passion and duty, selflessness and self-gratification, zeal for Jesus and zeal for rules. Just like Israel, I'm murky when it comes to my attitude and actions, sometimes getting it really wrong, other times genuinely pleasing the Lord. I'm blown away by His mercy with my inconsistency.

How tired I've grown of myself. I loathe my sin, especially the stuff I have on repeat. But God is faithful, always drawing me back to Himself, always forgiving the offense, always putting me back to work on Kingdom building, which of course, is the thing that matters—the thing that will have eternal value.

My heart's pendulum frequently sways between passion and duty, selflessness and self-gratification, zeal for Jesus and zeal for rules.

But grace is hard for me to accept. When I mess up again and again, I feel shame, which keeps me from running back to the Lord as quickly as I should. I'm just like Maya when she brings home a report card with mostly As, but she grieves the B. And no matter how much I tell her that I'm proud of her, that a B is wonderful and I don't care about grades anyway, that I'm so happy with her obvious effort and hard work and, quite frankly, the person she is, and that she should let it go and move on because I don't expect perfection, she still broods. She regrets. She "if onlys." And she gets stuck there.

The notion that our performance equals our worth is wrong and silly, and it's a lie from Satan. And Maya isn't the only one who buys it—I do too. Of course, try as I might, I'm not capable of a perfect score because I'm wired to mess up. I'm a sinner who needs a Savior, and there are times when I do much worse than Maya's B. I'm going to need to accept the ongoing gift of forgiveness and grace in order to keep walking, because missteps are a guarantee.

Not to mention the trouble I can count on that involves more than just me.

Our struggle is not against flesh and blood, but against the rulers, against the authorities, against the powers of this dark world and against the spiritual forces of evil in the heavenly realms. EPHESIANS 6:12

Mercy, the implications of that verse are hard to imagine. I spend half my time trying really hard to be good and the other half lamenting *not* being good, and I'm pretty sure I fail to recognize that there are outside forces at work. I'm so riddled with sin and evil desires that lead me astray that I rarely consider anything else. But while it's true that I'm responsible for my choices, it's helpful and necessary to know I'm being preyed upon. Satan and his minions know my weaknesses; they're well aware of the things that cause me to trip and fall and stay on the ground—which is all the more reason to cling to Jesus. I can't overcome the sin inside me, and on my own I'm defenseless against the wooing of our dark world. I should be terrified to go it alone, to obey in my own strength.

So my issues with obedience are many: my attitude is often bad even when my reasons are right, I frequently obey for the wrong reasons, I have a hard time accepting God's grace when I screw up, and I don't even recognize when the devil is in the details.

Oh—and I often judge people who aren't obeying as well as I perceive myself to be. Ha. I'm thinking my heavenly crown is going to be very light and lacking in bling.

But even now, as I sit here feeling forlorn by my lack of actual goodness, God is whispering in my ear to look up, to get my focus off the one who constantly gets it wrong and onto the one who never does, to fix my eyes on Him because He loves me unconditionally and longs to pour so much *right* into my mind that obedience will be abundant. He wants me to set my heart on my Savior, the one who welcomed Matt home a few weeks ago and who is, no doubt, listening to Matt's music echo through the corridors of heaven. I know that when my dear friend got there, he heard those unimaginably beautiful, soul-satisfying words, "Well done, my good and faithful servant."

Seven words worth living for, no doubt.

AWKWARD FOR JESUS

I rededicated my life to Christ when I was a freshman in college. Everything I had learned growing up and lukewarmly believed because my parents did came alive, and I was on fire. I couldn't get enough of apologetics or courses in Scripture or theological discussions. God was real to me in a way He hadn't been before, and I was all in. Sold. Down. Stick-a-fork-in-me done. Life had significant new meaning and purpose and focus, which always feels great . . . until something hard, or in my case, super awkward, comes around.

Late one Friday night when I was driving to my parents' house from campus, a car began to swerve from lane to lane in front of me. I eased off the gas as the zigzagging became more extreme, ultimately ending in a violent crash when the driver overcorrected and plowed into the shoulder wall—at, like, fifty miles an hour. I was the first witness on the scene, so I parked, ran to the car, and opened the passenger-side door. The inside was littered with beer cans and marijuana joints. Blood covered the woman's head, and she was crying and yelling at her wasted boyfriend behind the wheel whose eyes were open but unresponsive. I tried to keep her calm while we waited for the paramedics, who finally arrived and took over, though they asked me to stay and give a statement.

It seemed to take forever. A crowd gathered, and all of us just stood on the highway, our cars unattended. After watching the EMTs work for a while, I looked beyond the wreckage and saw two good-looking college-age guys. And then came that darn unmistakable still, small voice: "Go pray with them."

Um . . . what? *Surely I heard that wrong. I will assume I heard that wrong.*

But there it was again, like I was being tapped on the shoulder: "Go pray with them."

Lord, um, hello? What on earth are you saying? Pray with them? Those guys? No. No. No thank you, Lord.

Again: tap, tap. "Go pray with them."

Holy moly, Lord—that is a terrible idea.

But there it was again—*tap, tap, tap*, and it wasn't going away. *All right, God. Fine!*

I walked slowly around the wreckage and sidled up to the boys, who were tall and smelled good and dressed well.

Gulp.

"Um, hey guys. Pretty bad accident, huh?"

They looked around. It took a second for them to even realize I was talking to them. 'Cause why on earth would I be talking to them?

Sigh.

"So . . . uh . . . can I pray with you?"

Guy 1 said, "Pray? Uhhh . . . I guess. I mean, I used to be Catholic." Guy 2 just stared at me like I was insane.

"Okay, let's do it, then," I said. "Pray, I mean."

Ahem.

"Dear Lord, we pray for these people. Please help them. Please, um, help them. In Jesus' name, amen."

Ugh. So awkward. I think I actually thanked them before I walked back to the other side, where I remained in their line of vision until the cops finally took my statement. And here's the thing: I have no idea why God made me do it. There was no conversion on the side of the road, and I can't imagine my ridiculous prayer even planted a seed. I can only assume it was an exercise for my sake—a test of my newfound commitment to the Lord. Was He more important than my comfort level? Was I willing to obey, no matter how foolish I looked or felt? Was I really all in?

I was. Still am. I hope I don't have to be super awkward for Jesus very often, but I will when He asks. I want to be whatever He wants me to be because the older I get and the more sadness and hardship I witness and experience, the more I see Him at work, loving people, pouring out grace, and remaining faithful to sinful children who don't deserve it. He's worth being a fool for, worth sacrificing myself for, worth following into the desert for as long as He determines. He's worth dying to myself for. Worth turning my life upside down for. Worth growing in my capacity to give and receive grace for.

He's worth it.

So why should I obey? Because I truly am overwhelmed by the grace that will ultimately be my ticket into heaven. I'm starting to grasp a tiny inch of what grace really is and that it's an ocean we're invited to swim in every day. Like fresh water to a parched soul, grace replenishes my energy, willingness, and desire to follow Jesus. Grace is what should motivate my actions: I serve because I'm served by Jesus. I love because I'm loved by Jesus. I forgive because I'm forgiven by Jesus. I go because I'm carried. I rest because He provides it. I trust because He's faithful, time and time and time and time and time again. I offer myself as a living sacrifice because of His grace, and I pray to understand more and more the gift of God that is in Jesus Christ our Lord.

I serve because I'm served by Jesus. I love because I'm loved by Jesus. I forgive because I'm forgiven by Jesus. I go because I'm carried. I rest because He provides it.

Grace, grace, grace.

If I want to obey with my heart, not just my actions, I can't rely on my measly human strength. I need to rely on the Lord and His grace.

This is what the LORD says:
"Cursed are those who put their trust in mere humans,
  who rely on human strength
  and turn their hearts away from the LORD.
They are like stunted shrubs in the desert,
  with no hope for the future.
They will live in the barren wilderness,
  in an uninhabited salty land.

"But blessed are those who trust in the LORD
  and have made the LORD their hope and confidence.
They are like trees planted along a riverbank,
  with roots that reach deep into the water.
Such trees are not bothered by the heat
  or worried by long months of drought.
Their leaves stay green,
  and they never stop producing fruit."
JEREMIAH 17:5-8, NLT

God alone provides the wisdom, strength, and faith for us to continually obey no matter the circumstance. My silly prayer experience on the highway was, of course, nothing compared to other things I've been called to do, and certainly nothing compared to what I've seen others called to do. But the challenge it posed is the same in every situation: Am I willing to follow Jesus, anywhere and anytime? Do I trust His plan in all things, not just happy or easy things? Am I spending time with Him each day, allowing myself to be girded up for what lies ahead, including my need to receive grace and my ability to give it freely? And will I keep obedience in its proper place—as the outpouring of my love for Christ, not as a bargaining chip for an easier life or as justification for a sinful heart that breeds wrong motives?

Oh, Lord, make it so.

THE GOD WHO HEALS

After numerous delays on our drive to Kentucky, Dallas and I finally arrived at Matt's wake just before it was scheduled to end—to a line that wrapped through the halls of the church. We waited and waited and waited in that line, not wanting to play the BFF card for fear it would offend the people who'd been standing there longer than we had. But after an hour or so, someone recognized us and pulled us into the room where Ashley had been standing and greeting people for two days—more than three thousand visitors in all. I hadn't seen her in a year and honestly had no idea what to expect. Would she be stoic and in shock? Would she be a crumpled mess, unable to even stand? Would she be angry or irrational or terrified or permanently changed? I couldn't wait to get to her, to hug her and tell her that I loved her. But I was afraid, too, because I had no other words— nothing that could be of any value to a grieving wife and mother. I felt helpless, yet I had to get to her. I had to hug her and weep with her and remind her that she's not alone.

Because she's *not* alone. And not because I'm her friend or because her family is an extraordinary support system or because Southeast Christian Church has covered her with food and prayer and housecleaning and car maintenance. She's not alone, because God is by her side, closer than a brother, comforting her, carrying her, guiding her, and protecting her in the midst of the difficult circumstances He has called her to. For a fiercely, often painfully, devoted friend like me who doesn't live nearby and who worries for her friend every moment, it's been a remarkable thing to watch. Seeing God do what He does best has increased my faith because He is pouring out grace by the bucketful. Grace to put one foot in front of the other, grace to make the necessary financial decisions she now faces, grace to take care of her three young children and navigate their emotional trauma, grace to go through Matt's closet and drawers and know what to keep and what to give away, grace to forgive the man who didn't want to run over a bunny, grace to share the gospel with anyone who will listen, and grace to see people—including four of the nurses at the hospital where Matt was treated—give their lives to Jesus. She knows that God sustains. She has experienced it before and she's experiencing it now.

I'll never forget being in the room where Matt's body lay in an open casket, watching Ashley comfort the people who came intending to comfort her. Which is exactly what she did for me when I fell apart in her arms, shaking and weeping.

I asked her simply, "How are you doing this?"

She responded through tears and that faint, familiar smile, "The Lord."

CHAPTER 10

Diet Coke

SEPTEMBER 14

Time of day I usually crack my first can: 10 a.m.

Number I've had today and it's only noon: 3

Fountain of choice: Mickey Dees, large with extra ice, in the Styrofoam cup

Resolve to limit myself to two Diet Cokes and drink more water. Will start tomorrow. Or maybe the next day.

HEART OF DAVID

Krissie Cilano and her husband, Chuck, have been missionaries for close to two decades, and they're currently living in Thailand. When they first relocated from a thriving ministry in Italy, they couldn't even find Bibles in their area—the nearest available source was in Bangkok, which was a ten-hour drive. Six blessed years later, Chuck now operates two Christian bookstores with Bibles and books galore, produces and hosts a Christian radio program that broadcasts in two countries, brings in and leads short-term mission teams from other parts of Asia and the United States, teaches men's Bible studies, and preaches in numerous churches throughout the region.

And then there's Krissie, a full-time teacher at a local "Christian" school, where the faculty primarily consists of Buddhists and where they're required by law to teach Buddhism. When Krissie first arrived and requested a Bible—you know, because a Christian school usually supplies that sort of thing—they were hard pressed to track one down. In fact, the only tools at her disposal were two pieces of chalk, one board, and no desks, which meant her students had to sit on the floor in a stiflingly hot, noisy room. Not to mention that the woman working alongside Krissie had been teaching the students how to worship the rain.

But since Krissie's arrival (and post lots of prayer), the Lord has provided desks, dictionaries, bilingual Bibles, a PowerPoint projector, Internet access, and air-conditioning. She teaches English out of those bilingual Bibles to ten classes of fifty students each, as well as in all her other English classes at a nearby tech college. Students of all ages use the Bibles for vocabulary, spelling, story comprehension, and writing. The sixth graders memorize and recite Psalm 23 at their graduation each spring, a practice that is now considered tradition at the school. Oh, and the woman who worshiped water just got saved.

Needless to say, the Cilanos are making Jesus known.

And it really should be Krissie writing a book, because she's brilliant and quirky and hilarious and has hundreds of mind-blowing stories about God's provision and protection on the mission field. Stories that if I didn't know her so well, I might find difficult to believe. Stories that usually belong to sisters and brothers who give their lives to spreading the gospel—the ones who experience the sufficiency of Christ and depend on Him for absolutely everything in a way the rest of us only read about. For example, a few years ago, Krissie and a neighbor were outside talking to each other over the four-foot concrete wall that separated their houses, when the woman started screaming in prayer-like panic, "Oh, Jesus, Jesus, Jesus!"

Krissie spun around to see a spitting cobra coming straight

for her, its head up in striking position. Come on, now—a cobra *in her yard*. I'm not sure I can come up with a more compelling reason for me to *not* serve Jesus abroad, but I suppose I shouldn't put that in writing 'cause y'all know that's exactly where I'll end up. Anyway, there they were in the backyard with a large venom-spitting snake, when Krissie heard that inaudible, calm voice inside her head saying, "With my God I can scale a wall" (Psalm 18:29), and she knew she was going up the wall in front of her before the snake did.

Her friend ran into the house while Krissie launched herself on top of the wall like a sixty-three-year-old superhero, knowing the snake would follow. Apparently she had previously seen one scale the side of a fence, latching onto a tree with ease once it reached the top. And since there were small children playing on the other side, she knew she couldn't just run for cover. So, armed with her verse and a dull garden tool, she jumped on top of the wall, herself now in striking position as the snake started up after her. Before she knew it, she had pinned its mouth against the concrete and was yelling for her friend to find something sharp, which she did, and together they chopped off the snake's head. In fact, they had to chop the snake into seven pieces because it continued to coil and flail.

Oh. My. Word.

Kill me now.

And then there was the time Krissie and Chuck were living and serving in Italy, where they hosted half a dozen missionary teams each year. Chuck really thought they needed a large vehicle to transport the teams, so when they saw a white Mercedes van while walking past a dealership, Chuck lightheartedly said, "That's exactly what we need for the teams."

Krissie responded, "Well, we have $6,000 USD, and only God can get you a Mercedes for that kind of money."

Gee, I wonder what happened next.

A week later the phone rang. It was a man in Torino who had heard the Cilanos were interested in buying a van, and he was looking to sell. Krissie asked about the price and the color, and the guy said, "Six thousand USD, and it's white."

Turns out it wasn't just the right color van, exactly the size they needed, and the amount of money they had to spend; it was a Mercedes van with only eighteen thousand miles on the odometer. The seller owned a funeral home and used it to drive families to and from the cemetery. He wanted to replace it with a newer model and just needed to get rid of the old one. Um, SOLD. The van ended up carrying teams to outreaches where hundreds of thousands of Bibles were distributed.

Only God, right?

But here's the best story, and one that's so miraculous it's hard to comprehend. In fact, Chuck and Krissie haven't told many people because it's just too out there, though it's also just too amazing not to include. I'm going to use Krissie's words because my cynical paraphrasing could never do it justice.

We were in Fort Lauderdale, Florida, in the days before cell phones. I told Chuck I'd take his van in for an oil change while he was away doing something else. I felt really happy about it because I'd found a coupon: coupon + fifteen dollars = oil change.

I drove to a place on Route 441. There wasn't much there at the time—a nearly abandoned strip mall, some pawnshops and car places, a check-cashing store, some bus stops. The serviceman told me the van would be ready in an hour or so. He took the keys and drove the van onto a lift.

It was fall, so I thought I'd take a walk rather than wait there, but when I stepped over the curb I realized I hadn't

brought my purse. How stupid, I thought. No money, no
way of getting in touch with Chuck or any neighbors. . . .
Now what?

I looked up into the bright blue sky and was thinking
it would all work out somehow. The clouds were enormous
white pillows. I got lost in them and knew God was right
there with me. I started feeling that He was going to show
Himself. I just knew it. Like maybe He was going to say,
"Hi, Krissie" or something like that right out of the sky.
It made me laugh to think about.

I walked along the road pretty far before turning back to
the service station. There seemed to be a lot of people waiting
at bus stops that day. I laughed because I didn't even have
bus fare, which was twenty cents, but what a beautiful time
of year to be out walking! It was a day that made me sing
out loud.

First I felt the wind coming at me, then I saw branches
bending. I saw some airborne dust and newspapers, and
then I watched a man chase his hat. By then I was knee
deep in leaves that were covering the road! I could hear
the people at the bus stops going on about the leaves.
Then the wind really kicked up and there were big piles
of leaves blowing everywhere. I raised my arms and called
out, "Lord, You are so good! You are so wonderful! I love
who You are to me!" I didn't care who was watching;
I was in a whirlpool of leaves under that sky, knowing
God was doing something delightful. I could feel it in
my bones.

So, who would believe—even I had to look twice—that
a ten-dollar bill blew right at me—right into my right hand?
I held it up and jokingly said, "Yes, Lord! All I need is five
more!" And before I knew it, a five was in my other hand!

*I knew He was laughing and handing it right to me in
the frenzy!*

*Some people must have seen me with the money, because
they started scrambling in the leaves, looking for money
too. I was laughing so hard I could hardly call out to them,
"This is all I need right now!"*

*I waved to them and took off down the road to get
the van. If my feet touched the ground, I don't remember
that part.*

End quote—so beautiful I'm smiling at my computer screen.
Extraordinary provision, right? And just in case you need me
to, I'm vouching for Krissie because she's a truth teller who serves
God and trusts Him to show up anytime and anywhere. And so
He does, proving again and again that her faith is well founded.
I've never known anyone like her, and I've never heard such incred-
ible firsthand stories of God's sufficiency.

Her experience with the cobra makes me think of Daniel in
the lions' den, but her heart reminds me of David's. She regularly
speaks psalm-like praise to the mighty God she's devoted to,
almost dancing as she goes about her business each day, thinking
nothing of looking foolish or being misunderstood. She wakes
up singing and truly meaning, "His mercies are new each morning," whereas I often struggle to be pleasant by noon. She lies
down at night praying prayers like, "In peace I will lie down and
sleep because you alone, O Lord, will keep me safe," whereas I
often fret and plan and power through. She's hopeful and joyful
and thankful and seemingly fearless in the face of serious challenges, whereas I can be negative, discontent, and racked with
worry in my temperature-controlled, well-built, and stocked-
with-more-food-than-I-need home in the first-world country
where I live.

And if all her *wonderful* isn't enough, Krissie also eats the way she lives. During our two-week stay in Thailand, I couldn't get enough Tom Yum soup (amazing—had to have it) or chicken fried rice (way better there than here). But most of all I was losing my mind and craving Diet Coke, continually trying to fool my mouth into believing Thailand's version of Coke Zero sufficed. But Krissie would drink coconut milk or whatever other non-habit-forming thing was available because she's always just so happy to be alive and doesn't need anything in

> *I can be negative, discontent, and racked with worry in my temperature-controlled, well-built, and stocked-with-more-food-than-I-need home in the first-world country where I live.*

particular except for Jesus Christ her Lord and Savior; and my sarcasm is rearing its head because I can't understand how someone is so content all the time. More than that, I can't understand how a person depends on the Lord in every situation—for every breath—while I'm pretty sure I need another Diet Coke to make it through the day.

And also some other stuff.

NOT-SO-HOLY CRUTCHES

To be honest, Diet Coke isn't my only vice. I have plenty more in my daily repertoire, like the green tea I started drinking to *replace* Diet Coke but now just crave in addition to the Diet Coke. Or the quiet hour I feel desperate for every afternoon—so desperate that when I don't get it, it affects my mood for the rest of the day. Or my cleaning rituals that I obsess over because I want that peaceful feeling that comes when the dishes are put away and the pillows are fluffed and placed back in their proper positions on the couch—you know, that peaceful feeling that's threatened every time a kid dares to undo what I spent time doing. Or my uninterrupted TV time so I can watch all things Bravo, which I'm definitely ashamed of but not enough to stop watching *The Real Housewives of Any-City-Will-Do*. Or the attention I must have from my husband to feel human again after a long day with the kiddos.

And here's the truth about my list of "needs"—they aren't actually needs. They are, in fact, fine and good and harmless when kept in their proper place, meaning they're things I have freedom to do in moderation, when I have the time or energy to invest.

But they shouldn't be a substitute for relying on God, and they shouldn't supersede the needs of people around me—which they clearly have. Without them, I become angry, impatient, resentful, and self-pitying because after all, I deserve them, don't I? I need them because we women so often forget to take a moment for ourselves . . . right? At least that's what I keep hearing from *InStyle*, *O*, and every daytime talk show.

The truth is, I'm afraid to write this chapter because I don't want to give up my little indulgences—I want things the way I want them. I'm Sally in *When Harry Met Sally*, high maintenance and demanding without Meg Ryan's adorableness or quirky charm. I really like reality TV and watching wealthy women act insane. I want my house to be just so. I must have some time alone. And I love Diet Coke, but I definitely wonder if I love it too much. No question I'm addicted to the caffeine, as the headache comes by noon if I don't get my fix. But I don't think the Lord is convicting me to give it up altogether; I think He's convicting me to stop using it wrongly. And by that I mean drinking in excess or as a coping mechanism or as my source of peace.

I don't think the Lord is convicting me to give it up altogether; I think He's convicting me to stop using it wrongly.

I know it might sound ridiculous to label Diet Coke as a source of peace, but I'm pretty sure that's how I sometimes use it—as my own little escape or twist on comfort food. When I was in Thailand, I *craved* peace in the midst of our crazy circumstances, and I'd feel a twinge of it when I ordered stupid Coke Zero (for some reason, Diet Coke was impossible to find). But Max kept grabbing for it, and because I was trying to connect with my new little boy, I kept sharing. And while it sounds ridiculous, it was really hard to share because there were no free refills, and it took FOR-EV-ER to get the people behind the counter to understand I wanted extra ice. Each time I ordered, it was a big ordeal that included charades and unnecessary volume. "MORE ice, please. NO, not regular Coke. MOOOOORE ice. Chomp, chomp, chomp—you know, ICE? Brrrrr, cold—ice?! MOOOORE, please, MOOOORE—oh, for grief's sake."

Of course, I know that Jesus is supposed to be enough and that I won't actually die without Diet Coke or any of the other things that make me momentarily happy. But once again, what I know and what I experience are sometimes different. Jesus is supposed to be my portion and my cup and all that. But when I'm stressed, tired, or sad, He doesn't seem to scratch the itch as instantly as my silly list of favorite things. But I know the whole reason I need to depend on God is because Diet Coke doesn't satisfy for any longer than the time it takes to drink it, and the hour I spend with the housewives provides laughs and gasps, not peace. Obviously.

So how do I become more like Krissie? Is she blessed with a sweeter, more thankful, optimistic disposition that makes it easier to rely on God? Am I stuck with my type A, high-maintenance, everything-has-to-be-perfect-for-me-to-be-happy mentality that wars with my ability to rely on God? How can I enjoy the good things in life without subconsciously mistaking them for things I need to stay sane?

On the other hand, maybe I'm making too much of my crutches. After all, I'm not an alcoholic, shopaholic, sexaholic, or food addict. Doesn't God care more about the biggies? Surely my perfectionism run amuck and the little pick-me-ups I need to keep my emotions in check and my life in order aren't as bad as other people's stuff. Or does God actually want me to give up the things that have become too important?

Please say no, please say no . . .

PRACTICING DEPENDENCE

I'm sitting here on my couch pondering it all, wondering just how hard-core dependent I must become to please the Lord, and my thoughts have turned to fasting. More accurately, God is turning my attention to fasting—a topic I've mostly tried to avoid until this moment.

Because I really like to eat.

I've always assumed the purpose of fasting is to show God that I really, really mean what I pray . . . though I've only actually done it once. After years of prayer for a friend's salvation and zero visible change, I decided to plead my case to Jesus by going hungry for one day. With every hunger pain, I prayed. It felt long and hard and I gutted it out, which I was certain was the point—I was uncomfortable and the Lord knew it, so I made my case in heaven and got my friend a little closer to the pearly gates.

But if that were true, wouldn't my prayers have become less effective when I resumed eating the next day? I'm pretty sure I can't bribe God into answering my prayers. I can't pray harder or sweat more or plead loud enough to make God change what He's already going to do. He has a plan, and in some supernatural, unexplainable way, my prayers factor into His plan and make me part of it. But I'm pretty sure prayer is prayer. And by that I mean, the words I lift up while I'm feeding my family or driving to Costco are as heard by God as the ones I pray when I'm hungry and fasting.

Which begs the question: What's the point? And why am I even talking about fasting in a chapter called Diet Coke? Because God is showing me that fasting has two purposes: first, it's an opportunity to practice dependence—a practical exercise in trusting God's sufficiency. After all, for someone like me who loves to eat and to drink large amounts of Diet Coke, it takes a lot of dependence on the Lord to choose not to. And dependence starts with the little things, so when I place my dependence on something other than God, it becomes less instinctual to trust God in the bigger things. Second, fasting is a demonstration of my belief that God is sufficient—an act of faith that acknowledges His power, love, and faithfulness are enough to handle the circumstances and people I can't. He's bigger than the things that worry me, bigger than any roadblock in my way, and bigger than my hunger pains. Fasting is a powerful way for me to acknowledge and experience what I already believe. It's a physical representation of what happens in the spiritual realm—that God sustains and upholds and is sovereign over all things.

> *God is bigger than the things that worry me, bigger than any roadblock in my way, and bigger than my hunger pains.*

Jesus was led by the Spirit into the wilderness to be tempted there by the devil. For forty days and forty nights he fasted and became very hungry.

During that time the devil came and said to him, "If you are the Son of God, tell these stones to become loaves of bread."

But Jesus told him, "No! The Scriptures say,

'People do not live by bread alone,
but by every word that comes from the mouth of God.'"

Then the devil took him to the holy city, Jerusalem, to the highest point of the Temple, and said, "If you are the Son of God, jump off! For the Scriptures say,

> *'He will order his angels to protect you.*
> *And they will hold you up with their hands*
> *   so you won't even hurt your foot on a stone.'"*

Jesus responded, "The Scriptures also say, 'You must not test the LORD your God.'"

Next the devil took him to the peak of a very high mountain and showed him all the kingdoms of the world and their glory. "I will give it all to you," he said, "if you will kneel down and worship me."

"Get out of here, Satan," Jesus told him. "For the Scriptures say,

> *'You must worship the LORD your God*
> *   and serve only him.'"*

Then the devil went away, and angels came and took care of Jesus.

MATTHEW 4:1-11, NLT

Jesus went into the desert because He was led by the Holy Spirit to be tempted—but why did He also fast? He wasn't sweating blood and praying His guts out the way He did in the garden of Gethsemane—at least, it doesn't say that in the text. While the passage has implications for prayer, it doesn't directly teach us how to pray. What it does show is that Jesus was relying on God for strength as He dealt with temptation far greater than anything I'll ever know.

From a human perspective, it seems like fasting would've

made Him weak and, therefore, easier prey. But it appears to be the opposite. Jesus was practicing the dependence that would get him through the desert, his three-year ministry, and ultimately the Cross. The Father would need to be Jesus' only source of sufficiency time and time again, as Jesus would be hungry and tired and weak and persecuted and totally poured out. In His humanity, He would need to rely on the Father every moment of every day. And that total dependence started with fasting in the desert.

For all my striving to be better, healthier, more disciplined, more thankful, more content, and more perfect, and for all my temporary solutions when I'm running on fumes, God remains the source of all I need. *All I need.* I should be looking to Him for the things I lack, whether that's patience in the moment or peace in the storm or strength to make it till bedtime. The silly things like TV and food and Diet Coke are just that—silly things. He's the source of everything I actually need, and His rest, peace, and supernatural provision are available around the clock.

> *The LORD is my shepherd;*
> *I have all that I need.*
> *He lets me rest in green meadows;*
> *he leads me beside peaceful streams.*
> *He renews my strength.*
> *He guides me along right paths,*
> *bringing honor to his name.*
> *Even when I walk*
> *through the darkest valley,*
> *I will not be afraid,*
> *for you are close beside me.*
> *Your rod and your staff*
> *protect and comfort me.*
> *You prepare a feast for me*

in the presence of my enemies.
You honor me by anointing my head with oil.
My cup overflows with blessings.
Surely your goodness and unfailing love will pursue me
all the days of my life,
and I will live in the house of the LORD
forever.

PSALM 23:1-6, NLT

The things I enjoy become a problem when I exalt them as gods—specifically when I'm driven to have them more than I'm driven to spend time with and rely on the Lord. And that makes me pause for a moment to consider: *Is* my drive for Diet Coke greater, more palpable, more passionate than my drive to get alone with God every day? Practically speaking, I have to say yes. I can't wait to have my Diet Coke—I have to work hard to hold out until midmorning for my first can. The same is not true of my time with God. When I'm doing well with my quiet times, I open my Bible first thing in the morning before the kids are even awake. But for sure it's more of a discipline than a craving.

> *The things I enjoy become a problem when I exalt them as gods—specifically when I'm driven to have them more than I'm driven to spend time with and rely on the Lord.*

When I know I have one of my favorite shows DVRed, I think about it and look forward to sitting down, folding laundry, and watching. Not so with my time in the Word or in prayer. Ugh, that realization makes me sad, and it must be remedied, but is it possible for time with God to become my favorite thing? It's necessary and rewarding, of that I have no doubt. It directs my thoughts, my attitude, and my day. But when it comes to my emotions, my time with God is often in the same category as eating my vegetables or paying the bills—I feel great afterward, and my body and house run better as a result, but I don't ache to get right back to it. And I really, really want that to change because strength and joy come from spending time in His throne room. It's bizarre that I wouldn't want to be there as often as humanly possible or that a perfectionist like me would settle for artificial flavor.

ANTI-ROGUE

My pastor recently spoke about the story of Moses begging God to go with him and the Israelites as they made their way from Mount Sinai to the Promised Land. The problem was that God was angry with the people because while Moses was being given the Ten Commandments, the people were back at camp making and worshiping idols. Of course, up to that point, they'd been miraculously rescued by God from slavery in Egypt and led through the desert by a cloud during the day and a pillar of fire by night—the very presence of God. And they were being fed manna from the sky to the tune of no one going hungry in the wilderness. But Moses had been on that mountain for so long, and they apparently had an itch they were certain needed to be scratched right then and there. When Moses came down the mountain with words from God Himself, he saw all kinds of crazy and revelry and a great big golden calf.

So God said He was done with the Israelites, which completely freaked Moses out.

> One day Moses said to the LORD, "You have been telling me, 'Take these people up to the Promised Land.' But you haven't told me whom you will send with me. You have told me, 'I know you by name, and I look favorably on you.' If it is true that you look favorably on me, let me know your ways so I may understand you more fully and continue to enjoy your favor. And remember that this nation is your very own people."

The LORD replied, "I will personally go with you, Moses, and I will give you rest—everything will be fine for you."

Then Moses said, "If you don't personally go with us, don't make us leave this place. How will anyone know that you look favorably on me—on me and on your people—if you don't go with us? For your presence among us sets your people and me apart from all other people on the earth."

The LORD replied to Moses, "I will indeed do what you have asked, for I look favorably on you, and I know you by name."

Moses responded, "Then show me your glorious presence."

The LORD replied, "I will make all my goodness pass before you, and I will call out my name, Yahweh, before you. For I will show mercy to anyone I choose, and I will show compassion to anyone I choose. But you may not look directly at my face, for no one may see me and live." The LORD continued, "Look, stand near me on this rock. As my glorious presence passes by, I will hide you in the crevice of the rock and cover you with my hand until I have passed by. Then I will remove my hand and let you see me from behind. But my face will not be seen." EXODUS 33:12-23, NLT

When it came to relying on God in all things, Moses knew the drill. He was so terrified by the thought of going somewhere without the Lord that he didn't even hear God say, "I will personally go with you, Moses, and I will give you rest." He full-on missed it the first time because panic had set in. And after God repeated it, Moses wanted the reassurance of seeing God's presence, as he had in the form of the cloud and the pillar of fire. Of course, he didn't know what he was asking, and God allowed him to see as much glory as Moses could handle without keeling over dead.

It's a pretty extraordinary story, with a powerful application. Just like Moses, I should be terrified to do anything without the Lord. I should be constantly relying on His presence, His leading, and His protection. I should be terrified to go through my day without holding His hand and leaning hard into Him for strength. Why on earth do I continually settle for my own empty tank? I'm constantly running on the fumes of my own resources, losing my temper, tantruming in my heart, and shortchanging the people around me as I seek to self-protect and renew my *own* strength in really stupid ways, which is not a good plan—and Moses knew better. Like Krissie, he had seen too much of God's handiwork to settle for stupid.

But some habits are hard to break. On more than one occasion I've heard Dr. Phil say we shouldn't white-knuckle our way through life—meaning we can *will* something to work for a little while, but eventually we run out of steam, whether we're dieting, trying to control our tempers, battling addictions, or what have you. He suggests that whenever we want to stop a behavior, we should replace it with a new, healthier behavior—which is a biblical model for behavior modification. In other words, if I'm relying on something other than God, I must stop the misuse, turn from it, and replace it with Him.

And so, I'm going to pray at the beginning of every day that God would remove my cravings for the things that have become too important, that He would grant self-control, that He would enable me to turn to Him for peace, that I would seek long-term rest instead of relying on things that flee, and that I would keep fun things in their proper place—holding them loosely and refusing to allow them to dictate whether or not I have the perfect day.

And I'm going to refocus on the ever-important main thing.

You must love the LORD your God with all your heart, all your soul, and all your mind. This is the first and greatest commandment. MATTHEW 22:37-38, NLT

Of all the commandments Moses delivered to the people, Jesus said the most important is to love God with all I am, which means I should probably limit my Diet Coke intake along with all things Bravo because water and civility are good for me and I'm supposed to be a good steward of my mind and body. At the same time, I'm not going to overspiritualize things the Bible doesn't specifically address because I don't want to miss the point, which again, is to love God with all I am.

So I must learn to rely on the Lord, not on fleeting indulgences, for patience, strength, and perseverance. I have freedom for silly things, as long as they don't rule over me. Which begs one final question: Do my favorite things rule over me?

Yep.

So withdrawal is on the horizon.

THE MIRACLE OF SPEECHLESS

Most people who know me know I can talk—a lot—and so can Krissie, which means that together we could mow down an introvert in no time at all. On the streets of Thailand our chatter was so loud and animated, we frequently got glares—the Thai tend to be such quiet people. But it was worth the negative attention because Dal and I got to hear so many incredible stories from Krissie that made us laugh and cry, drop our jaws, and grow in our faith. We have so much respect and love for the Cilanos that we gave our newly adopted son their name (Max Cilano Jenkins), and our children will forever address them as aunt and uncle.

Guess you could say we adopted them, too.

In a recent e-mail exchange, dear Krissie wrote:

Believe me, I knew less than nothing about what to do when our ministry in Thailand started. I asked God to "show me," and He continues to inspire, direct, and refresh me.

The students are learning to speak, read, write, and listen to English; their scores are up, we're told. We hold Scrabble competitions and spelling bees, and right now I'm coaching a student who will enter an English speech contest. We invite students from other schools for a day of English Camp. It's very popular, especially among students who have friends in other schools. Even at these events we bring out the bilingual Bibles.

If you check a map, you will see that we are surrounded by communist countries that are not congenial to Bibles or to Christianity. God is so amazing. When He wants His Word into the hands of people, He knows how to make it happen. We are so privileged and humbled to be doing His will, and we are honored and blessed to have stories to tell.

And I'm pleased to report that God is gradually making me more like Aunt Krissie, with her unabashed confidence that He'll come through and that whatever He chooses will be sufficient. I know that God alone has the power to change my perfectionist heart, to silence the crazy voice inside my head, and to satisfy the cravings that beg for instant gratification. He's proving again and again that He's sufficient for all I need, be it food or drink or strength or peace.

He's all I need.

[Jesus] said to them, "I have food to eat that you know nothing about."

Then his disciples said to each other, "Could someone have brought him food?"

"My food," said Jesus, "is to do the will of him who sent me and to finish his work." JOHN 4:32-34

CHAPTER 11 ⫿⫿⫿⫿ Happiness

Things I still want to be when I grow up: 5

Things I hope to avoid like the plague: 5

Resolve to make the most of each day, to live well, and to die without regret.

SORORITY SISTERS

Like I said, I coteach a group of girls who attend Loyola Marymount University—sorority girls, that is, and they fit the bill. They're gorgeous, popular, and trendy. They do their fair share of partying (we're working on that), end sentences with words like *seriously* and *totally*, and don't just laugh—they LOL.

But these girls aren't exactly cliché. They're smart. Driven. They work their tails off and land exclusive internships. They're committed. They show up to Bible study every Monday night in spite of tests they need to study for and papers due the next day because they want to learn. They invite their friends to our study, and they invite us teachers to their fabulous events. They genuinely love each other, and I've come to genuinely love them. They ask us to pray for them, and they're starting to pray for each other. The experience of leading them has been wild, humbling, and deeply rewarding.

That said, I'm discovering the very large difference between college girls and me. Life through their eyes is limitless and, for the most part, exciting. They have lofty career goals and ambitious ten-year plans. They're romantics—some still waiting for Mr. Right, some working hard to hold on to him until graduation. And whatever the scenario, it includes living happily ever after.

Don't get me wrong. I'm not a cynic, and for the most part, I'm still a lot like them. I'm an optimist at heart, and I still dream about what the future may hold. But along with my thirties came a larger dose of reality than I had previously experienced. I've seen friends divorce, struggle to get pregnant, endure multiple miscarriages, get sick and walk out of the hospital with a colostomy bag, lose jobs, change careers, struggle financially, remain single in spite of eHarmony, lose children to cancer, lose parents to Alzheimer's, and the list goes on.

I sometimes miss my college days, when my biggest concerns were doing homework and making time for social events—which is exactly how college should be. It's not real life; it's a transition to real life. Since reality has a tendency to be less than ideal, I certainly wouldn't wish it on my Delta Gamma girls prematurely. Heck, I don't wish it on my grown-up self either. Which is the reason I'm putting *annual family pass to Disneyland* on my Christmas wish list this year.

MY HAPPY PLACE

I love Disneyland. Always have. I remember driving there as a kid from our home in Santa Clarita. The closer we got to the park, the prettier everything became. More trees, more flowers, wider lanes. Ever since then, when I see lush green plants along a clean, well-groomed stretch of highway, I'm reminded of Disneyland and all its glory.

Of course, the actual park is way better than the drive in. Vibrant colors, helpful workers, music-filled streets delivered by Dapper Dans, horse-drawn trolley cars, fabulous smells, familiar sights, and the fantastical castle that represents the magic we grew up with. My favorite moment is always the walk down Main Street on the way into the park. So much to see and do, and always the promise of a perfect day in a perfect place.

And my intoxication is no accident. In recent years Dallas and I have spent time with a former Disney Imagineer—the official job title for the guys who design Disney theme parks. (Possibly the coolest job ever.) Turns out everything we see, hear, and smell (and everything we don't) in Disneyland is designed to create and maintain the magic. The bakery ovens vent onto Main Street for all passersby to smell. Every window in every shop is washed three times a day. The bushes, flowers, and trees are maintained or replaced at night when the park is closed. The staff enters and exits the park through an underground facility, where all costume changes and other staff-related activities take place. The trash cans sit on manholes so they can be emptied via the underground system. The outside world of hotels, malls, and freeways is not visible from anywhere in the park. And all of the above are intentionally designed to keep park goers in the excitement of the moment.

I wish life were more like Disneyland. I wish things were beautiful, colorful, and well kept all the time. I wish everyone were happy. I wish everything were clean and wrapped with a nice, neat bow. And of course, I wish dreams really would come true.

In other words, it takes an army of people and a serious game plan (not to mention lots and lots of money) to create the facade of perfection that is Disneyland. Of course, I didn't really need the inside scoop from my friend to know that a day in the Magic Kingdom isn't actually magical—to know that the trash still stinks, the employees' smiles aren't always genuine, and some of the princesses go barhopping after work. Because no matter how well it's hidden from park goers, the walk down Main Street at day's end tells the real story. Kids are worn out and whining, everyone's tired of fighting crowds, couples are bickering, wallets are empty, people are dirty and sweaty and sunburned, feet hurt, and overpriced souvenirs break before making it to the car.

Yet *done* as I usually am when we return home, I'm always a little sad, too, knowing it'll be a while before we can afford to go back. Because in spite of what I know to be true, I like suspending reality for just a moment on Main Street. And I've come to understand something about myself: no matter how ridiculous the notion, I wish life were more like Disneyland. I wish things were beautiful, colorful, and well kept all the time. I wish everyone were happy. I wish I were carefree and ready for adventure—adventure guaranteed to end well. I wish life were always kid friendly and safe. I wish everything were clean and wrapped with a nice, neat bow. And of course, I wish dreams really would come true.

I'm experienced enough to know that nothing is perfect, that even when happiness is rooted in the best of circumstances, it's unsustainable.

But back in reality (and in the heart of LA, no less), magic and perfection are out of reach, and instead messiness abounds. I long for a Disneyland existence and continue to strive for it, which drives my vanity, materialism, parenting, plans, and pride. They're all based on my pursuit of a happy, perfect life.

So what to do? I'm experienced enough to know that nothing is perfect and that even when happiness is rooted in the best of circumstances, it's unsustainable. Which makes me wonder:

How do faith and hope in God play a practical role in the decaying here and now? And by that I mean, what's God's response to the bestselling bumper sticker of all time—life is hard and then you die?

ORIGINAL PERFECT

In my opinion, there's no better way to understand our lives than to look back.

Way back.

> *The LORD God had planted a garden in the east, in Eden;*
> *and there he put the man he had formed. The LORD God*
> *made all kinds of trees grow out of the ground—trees that*
> *were pleasing to the eye and good for food. In the middle of*
> *the garden were the tree of life and the tree of the knowledge*
> *of good and evil.*
>
> *A river watering the garden flowed from Eden; from*
> *there it was separated into four headwaters. The name of*
> *the first is the Pishon; it winds through the entire land of*
> *Havilah, where there is gold. (The gold of that land is good;*
> *aromatic resin and onyx are also there.) The name of the*
> *second river is the Gihon; it winds through the entire land*
> *of Cush. The name of the third river is the Tigris; it runs*
> *along the east side of Ashur. And the fourth river is the*
> *Euphrates.*
>
> *The LORD God took the man and put him in the Garden*
> *of Eden to work it and take care of it. And the LORD God*
> *commanded the man, "You are free to eat from any tree*
> *in the garden; but you must not eat from the tree of the*
> *knowledge of good and evil, for when you eat from it you*
> *will certainly die."*
>
> GENESIS 2:8-17

I've always thought of Eden as an almost mythical place, separate from earth as we know it. And while that's partly true (in that no one's been there since Adam and Eve were booted out), it's of note that Eden is described geographically by the confluence of rivers that still exist today. In other words, it's a real place where real people really lived.

And it was awesome. I can only deduce that Disneyland has nothing on Eden. Trees of all kinds that were beautiful and produced fruit. Flowing rivers that watered everything in sight. Peace between God and nature and animals. Work was life giving, not a struggle. And there was true rest. Everything in harmony, just as God created it to be.

Until . . .

> *The serpent was more crafty than any of the wild animals the LORD God had made. He said to the woman, "Did God really say, 'You must not eat from any tree in the garden'?"*
>
> *The woman said to the serpent, "We may eat fruit from the trees in the garden, but God did say, 'You must not eat fruit from the tree that is in the middle of the garden, and you must not touch it, or you will die.'"*
>
> *"You will not certainly die," the serpent said to the woman. "For God knows that when you eat from it your eyes will be opened, and you will be like God, knowing good and evil."*
>
> *When the woman saw that the fruit of the tree was good for food and pleasing to the eye, and also desirable for gaining wisdom, she took some and ate it. She also gave some to her husband, who was with her, and he ate it. Then the eyes of both of them were opened, and they realized they were naked; so they sewed fig leaves together and made coverings for themselves.* GENESIS 3:1-7

Enter messiness and consequence. And so . . .

The man and his wife heard the sound of the LORD God
as he was walking in the garden in the cool of the day, and
they hid from the LORD God among the trees of the garden.
But the LORD God called to the man, "Where are you?"

He answered, "I heard you in the garden, and I was
afraid because I was naked; so I hid."

And he said, "Who told you that you were naked? Have
you eaten from the tree that I commanded you not to eat
from?"

The man said, "The woman you put here with me—she
gave me some fruit from the tree, and I ate it."

Then the LORD God said to the woman, "What is this
you have done?"

The woman said, "The serpent deceived me, and I ate."

GENESIS 3:8-13

Punishments were appropriately doled out. And then . . .

The LORD God made garments of skin for Adam and his
wife and clothed them. And the LORD God said, "The
man has now become like one of us, knowing good and
evil. He must not be allowed to reach out his hand and
take also from the tree of life and eat, and live forever." So
the LORD God banished him from the Garden of Eden to
work the ground from which he had been taken. After he
drove the man out, he placed on the east side of the Garden
of Eden cherubim and a flaming sword flashing back and
forth to guard the way to the tree of life.

GENESIS 3:21-24

Okay, a couple of things to note from Adam and Eve's story:

1. God created life to be perfect. Case in point: Eden was perfect.
2. God gave Adam and Eve the choice (in the form of a tree) to believe Him or to not believe Him.
3. From the first moment Adam and Eve chose to go their own way, guilt, shame, and brokenness were the result.
4. With defiance came consequences, including that Adam and Eve were removed from the Garden. But not because God was angry—quite the contrary. When Adam and Eve ate from the tree of the knowledge of good and evil, their relationship with God was broken. They couldn't be permitted to also eat from the tree of life because if they did, they would have lived forever in their broken, cursed state. And so, to protect them from spending an eternity in the mess they'd made, God drove them out and set a guard at the tree.
5. God made clothes, which is an easy part of the story to overlook, but it reveals something extraordinary. In the midst of this tragic moment, when relationship with God had been broken, God saw that Adam and Eve were embarrassed to be naked and were struggling to cover themselves—so He clothed them. He loved them and showed them mercy, even in their disbelief. He covered their sin and shame—a precursor to the Cross.

That was the beginning—the story of what life was supposed to be like and how it went terribly wrong, which is of note because it's no coincidence that the perfection I crave is exactly what God intended. Simply put, we were meant for more. But while God is the author of beauty and tranquility, we are the authors of ugliness and strife. We attempt to create beauty through our appearance, our relationships, and our abilities, and sometimes we experience a measure of success. The problem is that sooner or later all the things we create slip away via decay, neglect, or death. We simply can't maintain beauty. We are, in fact, at odds with it.

It's no coincidence that the perfection I crave is exactly what God intended.

Thankfully, through Christ's death we're given the opportunity to live, at least in part, the way we were intended to: in relationship with God and as stewards of our lives instead of as slaves to them.

> *My old self has been crucified with Christ. It is no longer I who live, but Christ lives in me. So I live in this earthly body by trusting in the Son of God, who loved me and gave himself for me.* GALATIANS 2:20, NLT

The things I cling to—my vices, my sins, my very life—were crucified with Christ when I decided to follow him. So why do they continue to direct my thoughts and actions? The answer is obvious: most days I don't live by faith. Most days I want immediate gratification, and in that pursuit, I put myself at the mercy of the world we broke, choosing snakes and apples over God and the Garden. So the question becomes, what does it look like to live by faith? And how would my life be different if I did?

Only one way to find out.

SKYWARD EYES

For my son Sam's first birthday, friends of ours gave him an inflatable ball contraption. It was huge—more than three feet tall and probably as wide. Brightly colored balls went in at the top, spiraled down a see-through tube, and landed in a pool of balls big enough for him to jump in. It was by far the coolest toy we'd ever owned.

Unfortunately for me, we didn't have an air pump. So while Sam waited for me to blow the thing up manually, he played in the dirt. By the time I finally finished, he was so fixated on what he was doing that he wouldn't turn around. I literally had to force him to look up, which of course made him cry. So there I was, pale and woozy, trying to give him this great new toy. "Look what Mommy made for you!" I told him, while he cried and cried, holding tight to a fistful of dirt and rocks.

> *Most days I want immediate gratification, and in that pursuit, I put myself at the mercy of the world we broke, choosing snakes and apples over God and the Garden.*

And I do the same ridiculous thing. I cling to dirt in all its forms, believing it will make me happy, while God pleads with me to look up. Because, of course, the only way to experience life the way God intends is to choose Him day by day, moment by moment. To resist the urge to cling to my appearance, my money, my plans, my pride, and my dreams—and instead to fix my eyes on Jesus. To rest in God's love, knowing I'm saved because of His grace and not because I'm perfect or even good. To pray for faith and courage enough to dive into the kind of life He wants for me.

Simply put, my choice is the same today as it was for Adam and Eve, and later for the Israelites who were looking ahead to the Promised Land: life or death, blessings or curses.

> *Today I have given you the choice between life and death, between blessings and curses. Now I call on heaven and earth to witness the choice you make. Oh, that you would choose life, so that you and your descendants might live!*
>
> DEUTERONOMY 30:19, NLT

And because the fight for our attention and allegiance rages on—
and the world continues to decay and disappoint—Paul said this:

*I once thought these things were valuable, but now I
consider them worthless because of what Christ has done.
Yes, everything else is worthless when compared with the
infinite value of knowing Christ Jesus my Lord. For his sake
I have discarded everything else, counting it all as garbage,
so that I could gain Christ and become one with him. I no
longer count on my own righteousness through obeying the
law; rather, I become righteous through faith in Christ.
For God's way of making us right with himself depends on
faith. I want to know Christ and experience the mighty
power that raised him from the dead. I want to suffer with
him, sharing in his death, so that one way or another I will
experience the resurrection from the dead!*
PHILIPPIANS 3:7-11, NLT

It's the lesson God has to teach me over and over—our prize
has nothing to do with earthly things. The very things we consider desirable, Paul considered rubbish compared to knowing and
growing in relationship with Jesus.

And he pursued knowing Jesus more.

*I don't mean to say that I have already achieved these things
or that I have already reached perfection. But I press on to
possess that perfection for which Christ Jesus first possessed
me. No, dear brothers and sisters, I have not achieved it, but
I focus on this one thing: Forgetting the past and looking
forward to what lies ahead, I press on to reach the end of the
race and receive the heavenly prize for which God, through
Christ Jesus, is calling us.* PHILIPPIANS 3:12-14, NLT

Like Paul—and my precious little boy—it's time to look up. It's time to live life with a new perspective and a different set of priorities. It's time to believe Jesus when He says, "*I am* the way and the truth and the life" (John 14:6, emphasis added). All other pursuits lead to disappointment and death, be it now or fifty years from now. All other hopes will be dashed. All dreams, whether realized or lost, will pass away. Jesus and the life He offers are eternal. Our only true happiness.

CHIN UP

Recently my footloose and fancy-free sorority girls have been anything but. One graduated last spring, only to find that her expectations of postcollege life were too high. Specifically, the boy (and I say *boy* with great intention) she'd been dating for three years wasn't ready to be serious, now or probably ever, so she ended it. And although she landed a great job with an impressive title (especially for one so young), most of her college friends have moved away and she's starting the next chapter of her life alone. Another girl just found out that her mom, grandpa, and cousin are all sick with cancer. She's understandably distracted and is currently deciding whether to leave school to help care for them. Another hasn't heard back from any of the postgraduate nursing programs she has applied to and is terrified she won't get in. Another girl's brother was quarantined with the H1N1 virus, and still another's newlywed big sister just had a seizure. Doctors are currently looking into possible causes, including a brain tumor.

And what is there to tell them but that life is imperfect? And of course that our only solace, whether in good times or in bad, is that someday creation will be restored. Someday no one will be sick. Someday there will be no more tears and no more fear. Someday we'll know true beauty. Someday there will be justice and peace and lions befriending lambs. Someday God will reign and everything will be perfect, the way He created it to be.

Because someday we'll see Eden.

> I saw "a new heaven and a new earth," for the first heaven and the first earth had passed away, and there was no longer any sea. I saw the Holy City, the new Jerusalem, coming down out of heaven from God, prepared as a bride beautifully dressed for her husband. And I heard a loud voice from the throne saying, "Look! God's dwelling place is now among the people, and he will dwell with them. They will be his people, and God himself will be with them and be their God. 'He will wipe every tear from their eyes. There will be no more death' or mourning or crying or pain, for the old order of things has passed away."
>
> He who was seated on the throne said, "I am making everything new!" Then he said, "Write this down, for these words are trustworthy and true."
>
> He said to me: "It is done. I am the Alpha and the Omega, the Beginning and the End. To the thirsty I will give water without cost from the spring of the water of life. Those who are victorious will inherit all this, and I will be their God and they will be my children. . . ."
>
> The angel showed me the river of the water of life, as clear as crystal, flowing from the throne of God and of the Lamb down the middle of the great street of the city. On each side of the river stood the tree of life, bearing twelve crops of fruit, yielding its fruit every month. And the leaves of the tree are for the healing of the nations. No longer will there be any curse. The throne of God and of the Lamb will be in the city, and his servants will serve

him. They will see his face, and his name will be on their
foreheads. There will be no more night. They will not
need the light of a lamp or the light of the sun, for the
Lord God will give them light. And they will reign for
ever and ever. REVELATION 21:1-7; 22:1-5

Now that's what I'm talkin' about.

CHAPTER 12 |||||||||| # Freedom

NOVEMBER 12

Here I am, a year and some months after my journey began, and while I've experienced some victory over my perfectionism, in many ways I'm still struggling—and my greatest wondering remains: Is it possible to ever really be free? And what does *freedom* even mean? I know my desire to be perfect in any category is mostly unattainable and always unsustainable . . . of that, I'm convinced. Yet I continually return to my pursuit of the impossible and all the sin that comes with it.

But I'm grateful to know I'm not alone. And it can't hurt to be reminded that even hard-core, gospel-spreading, willing-to-be-killed-for-Jesus Paul had a similar ongoing struggle with sin.

I know that nothing good lives in me, that is, in my sinful nature. I want to do what is right, but I can't. I want to do what is good, but I don't. I don't want to do what is wrong, but I do it anyway. But if I do what I don't want to do, I am not really the one doing wrong; it is sin living in me that does it.

*I have discovered this principle of life—that when I
want to do what is right, I inevitably do what is wrong.
I love God's law with all my heart. But there is another
power within me that is at war with my mind. This
power makes me a slave to the sin that is still within me.*
ROMANS 7:18-23, NLT

*In order to sustain
meaningful change in my
life, I must first understand
how not free I really am.*

A slave to sin—that sounds about
right. I often try willing myself to be
good—to stop being vain or materialistic
or whatever—because for short periods of
time, I actually can. For weeks I'll stick to
my budget, read my Bible, laugh at my
crow's-feet, and find my identity in Jesus.
But eventually I return to the things I tried leaving behind—"As a
dog returns to its vomit, so a fool repeats his foolishness" (Proverbs
26:11, NLT). And the bottom line is that in order to sustain meaningful change in my life, I must first understand how *not* free I
really am. Which is why I appreciate Mel Gibson—and by that I
mean, William Wallace.

If you haven't seen *Braveheart,* here's the skinny: Scotland was
invaded and conquered in 1296 by King Edward I of England,
and consequently Scots suffered abuse at the hands of English sol-
diers who raped and pillaged under the protection of English law.
William Wallace led the resistance against
the English, inspiring thousands to fight
alongside him in the name of freedom.

*Sin masquerades as all
things lovely and freedom
giving, but ultimately it
plunders, leaving my heart
and my life in ruins.*

And the analogy is that apart from
Christ I, too, am subject to tyranny. Only
instead of being ruled by a cruel king, I'm
ruled by sin, which seeks both my allegiance and my demise. Sin masquerades

as all things lovely and freedom giving, but ultimately it plunders, leaving my heart and my life in ruins. Like an occupying nation, sin settles in, allowing me to think I've got life under control. But eventually sin emerges and wields its power, and when it does, it's unyielding and unforgiving.

Of course, according to Scripture, the alternative to being ruled by sin is to be *free in Jesus*. But in the past year, I've realized I don't fully understand what spiritual freedom is because in my experience the way it's defined depends on where you live.

TURF WARS

I was raised in the Bible Belt culture of the Midwest, so I know what it means to be a "good" Christian—to say grace before taking a bite, to attend church rain or shine, to not drink or smoke or swear, and to avoid dancing and playing cards. On the other hand, I lived in LA for ten years, where the focus is less on being good and more on being "free in Christ, *man*," which for many means the freedom to get drunk, have premarital sex, get divorced, skip church, swear like sailors, and criticize the uptight, legalistic Christians who still think those things are wrong.

I don't think I'm going out on a limb to say that both extremes are missing the point and that freedom is often misunderstood. Before Jesus came, believers were required to follow a bunch of rules in order to be in relationship with God. Post Jesus, we're not. Yet I remain a perfectionist—a do-gooder—which is rooted in the belief that I must earn my worth, though Scripture teaches the opposite.

> *A person is not justified by the works of the law, but by faith in Jesus Christ. So we, too, have put our faith in Christ Jesus that we may be justified by faith in Christ and not by the*

works of the law, because by the works of the law no one will be justified. GALATIANS 2:16

God saved you by his grace when you believed. And you can't take credit for this; it is a gift from God. Salvation is not a reward for the good things we have done, so none of us can boast about it.
EPHESIANS 2:8-9, NLT

While it's true that salvation is by grace alone and that believers have been set free *from sin* as the result of that grace, we have not been set free. Let me say that again—we aren't free. When Scotland won its independence in 1314, its citizens were set free from English tyranny, but not from responsibility and certainly not from Scottish law. In the same way, when we accept Christ's gift of salvation, we're set free from the tyranny of sin and death, but the Bible says we have a new master.

Sin is no longer your master, for you no longer live under the requirements of the law. Instead, you live under the freedom of God's grace.
Well then, since God's grace has set us free from the law, does that mean we can go on sinning? Of course not! Don't you realize that you become the slave of whatever you choose to obey? You can be a slave to sin, which leads to death, or you can choose to obey God, which leads to righteous living. Thank God! . . . Now you are free from your slavery to sin, and you have become slaves to righteous living.
ROMANS 6:14-18, NLT

Let the Holy Spirit guide your lives. Then you won't be doing what your sinful nature craves. The sinful nature wants to

*do evil, which is just the opposite of what the Spirit wants.
And the Spirit gives us desires that are the opposite of what
the sinful nature desires. These two forces are constantly
fighting each other, so you are not free to carry out your good
intentions. But when you are directed by the Spirit, you are
not under obligation to the law of Moses.*

*When you follow the desires of your sinful nature, the
results are very clear: sexual immorality, impurity, lustful
pleasures, idolatry, sorcery, hostility, quarreling, jealousy,
outbursts of anger, selfish ambition, dissension, division,
envy, drunkenness, wild parties, and other sins like these.
Let me tell you again, as I have before, that anyone living
that sort of life will not inherit the Kingdom of God.*

*But the Holy Spirit produces this kind of fruit in
our lives: love, joy, peace, patience, kindness, goodness,
faithfulness, gentleness, and self-control. There is no law
against these things!*

*Those who belong to Christ Jesus have nailed the passions
and desires of their sinful nature to his cross and crucified
them there. Since we are living by the Spirit, let us follow
the Spirit's leading in every part of our lives.*

GALATIANS 5:16-25, NLT

In Jesus I'm free *from* and free *to*. Free from sin and death,
free from the law that indicts me, and free from having to earn
my salvation. I'm also free to love God, to approach Him without
fear, to serve wholeheartedly, and to be grown and changed by the
Holy Spirit. But I'm not autonomous. I don't get to be queen for
even one day. And the two masters vying for my patronage are sin
in all its forms and the God who loves me.

DEFYING TYRANNY

It's been said that the real William Wallace lived and died by his uncle's creed:

> *This is the truth I tell you:*
> *of all things freedom's most fine.*
> *Never submit to live, my son,*
> *in the bonds of slavery entwined.*

When I see sin for what it is, choosing God and His brand of freedom (love, joy, peace, patience, etc.) is a no-brainer. But the temptation to sin remains, and I'm weak and easily led astray, so I need to channel my inner William Wallace. I must learn to defend my freedom.

> *Be strong in the Lord and in his mighty power. Put on all of God's armor so that you will be able to stand firm against all strategies of the devil. For we are not fighting against flesh-and-blood enemies, but against evil rulers and authorities of the unseen world, against mighty powers in this dark world, and against evil spirits in the heavenly places.*
> *Therefore, put on every piece of God's armor so you will be able to resist the enemy in the time of evil. Then after the battle you will still be standing firm. Stand your ground, putting on the belt of truth and the body armor of God's righteousness. For shoes, put on the peace that comes from the Good News so that you will be fully prepared. In addition to all of these, hold up the shield of faith to stop the fiery arrows of the devil. Put on salvation as your helmet, and take the sword of the Spirit, which is the word of God.*
> *Pray in the Spirit at all times and on every occasion.*

*Stay alert and be persistent in your prayers for all believers
everywhere.* EPHESIANS 6:10-18, NLT

The best defense is a good offense, which is true in athletics
and in life. I find that when I let my spiritual guard down, the
enemy seizes the opportunity. So the key to victory and freedom
is simple: be ready.

1. **Put on the belt of truth.** I need to know and believe
   what the Bible says about sin. I need to get real with
   myself and with others in regard to the hold sin has on
   my life. I need to be accountable. I need to confess when
   I fail. I need to remember what Christ has done to defeat
   sin, and I need to know and believe what the Bible says
   about grace. I need to bask in the knowledge that I'm
   forgiven and made new in Jesus. I need to understand
   that I'm a sinner, in desperate need of a Savior, and
   through my Savior's sacrifice, I'm an heir in the
   Kingdom of God.

2. **Put on the body armor of God's righteousness.** I need
   to follow in the footsteps of my Savior, believing His way
   is best. I need to remember that I have no righteousness
   apart from Christ, and that the good in me—my ability
   to choose well *ever*—is because of the power of the Holy
   Spirit working in and through me. I need to love the
   things God loves and pursue the things God pursues.
   I need to embrace the light of God's Word in my life,
   no matter what it exposes or how humbling it may be.
   I should desire holiness and the methods God employs
   to bring me closer to it. I should desire that God be
   glorified in my life and choices.

God has overcome the world and all its yuckiness, and therefore fear has no place in my life.

3. **Put on the shoes of peace.** I need to remember that no matter what I've done (or may do), Christ's death on the cross bridges the gap between me and God—I'm forgiven. I need to believe that God is the Good Shepherd who takes care of me, a sheep He loves and knows by name. I need to remember that God has overcome the world and all its yuckiness, and therefore fear has no place in my life. And I need to be an ambassador of the peace I have in Jesus—to proclaim what I know and what I've found to people in desperate need of hearing it. After all, these boots, I mean shoes, were made for walkin'.

4. **Hold up the shield of faith.** I need to hope in things I don't see yet, like answers to unanswered prayer and heaven. I need to remind myself of what I know and have experienced of God—that He's good, loving, and faithful. I need to learn a lesson from the Battle of Stirling Bridge, portrayed in *Braveheart*. When the English army charges the battlefield, swords drawn, horses running at full speed toward the much smaller Scottish resistance, the freedom fighters stand their ground, swords at their sides, while Wallace yells, "Hold! . . . Hold! . . . Hold!" At the last moment, and when it is too late for the English to stop, the Scots pick up their spears, anchor them, and take out the entire opposing front line—and I, too, need to hold the line. To believe in the face of adversity that God knows what He's doing. To trust that His plan for my life is right. To resist the doubt that rears its head when things get tough and the enemy is bearing down.

5. **Put on the helmet of salvation.** I need to guard my mind
with Christ—to filter all things incoming with truth.
I once heard a pastor say that whether we're insecure
or prideful, we're guilty of not defining ourselves by
the gospel. In other words, I'm a sinner saved by grace,
so pride has no place in my life. I'm also an heir in the
Kingdom of God, an adopted child loved beyond what I
can comprehend, so insecurity has no place in my life. My
identity is supposed to be in Jesus, and everything I do,
desire, and believe should be rooted in Him. I must take
captive the thoughts that are not in step with the gospel.

6. **Take the sword of the Spirit—God's Word.** I need to read
the Bible and live my life according to what it says. I need
to make time for God every day, knowing it's easy to
forget the truth of Scripture and go my own way. I need
to be bold in the face of culture, refusing to conform to
its values. I must allow God's Word to cut through the
lies I'm tempted to believe. I must cling to the truth and
proclaim it so others might also hear and believe.

So is it possible to really be free from perfectionism, from the
pressure of our beauty-, money-, and status-obsessed culture, and
from the strangleholds I've succumbed to? It is—as long as I follow
God, suited for battle. And as long as I pursue the *right* brand of
perfection, which is to be conformed to the image of Jesus Christ,
my prize.

*I don't mean to say that I have already achieved these things
or that I have already reached perfection. But I press on to
possess that perfection for which Christ Jesus first possessed
me. No, dear brothers and sisters, I have not achieved it,*

but I focus on this one thing: Forgetting the past and looking forward to what lies ahead, I press on to reach the end of the race and receive the heavenly prize for which God, through Christ Jesus, is calling us. PHILIPPIANS 3:12-14, NLT

New Chapter

Status: Hugely imperfect and starting to be okay with it

Strangleholds: Not to brag, but definitely fewer than last year

Hopes: Closing in on 1

*Resolve to know my Maker and to look to Him for my worth;
to care less about my image and more about my impact; to fight
temptation, live in truth, be transparent, and love what God
loves; to trust God with the people in my life who matter most;
to press on when I fail and praise God when I don't; to embrace
my imperfection and to set my eyes on God's perfection.
Resolve to live free in Jesus.*

Discussion Questions

For Bible study, small groups, books clubs—what have you . . . it's your turn.

As you discuss these questions, I encourage you to be honest with yourself, with the people around you, and with the Lord about your *own* journey because there's freedom in transparency. Remember, every teacher says the same thing—"If you're struggling with something, the people around you are probably struggling too," which is true in school and in life. And there's encouragement and accountability in numbers.

Refuse to hide.

Refuse to let Satan keep you isolated in your sin and struggle.

Believe Jesus when He says the truth will set you free (John 8:31-32).

Telling the truth gets easier the more you do it—trust me, I know. Because when you realize that you're not alone and that God has provided everything you need in His Word, strangleholds get loosed, and intimacy between you and the Lord begins to thrive.

And it doesn't get better than that.

Happy confessing, dear reader.

CHAPTER 1 |||||||||| Vanity ═══

The LORD said to Samuel, "Do not consider his appearance
or his height, for I have rejected him. The LORD does not
look at the things people look at. People look at the outward
appearance, but the LORD looks at the heart."
1 SAMUEL 16:7

1. How much time do you spend thinking about or talking
   about your body each day? What flaws do you fixate on?

   _____

   _____

2. How do you respond—inwardly and outwardly—to
   someone who looks the way you want to look?

   _____

   _____

3. Read 1 Corinthians 6:12-20. What does it mean to take
   care of our bodies in the context of the passage? What is the
   general principle we can apply about how God wants us to
   treat our bodies?

   _____

   _____

4. Where's the line between vanity and taking care of your
   body because it's the temple of the Holy Spirit?

   _____

   _____

5. How would your life be different if you were clothed in strength and dignity?

_____

_____

6. Read Psalm 139:13-14. What are three attributes _unique to you_ that make you beautiful in God's eyes?

_____

_____

7. How can you use what God has given you to glorify Him and further His Kingdom?

_____

_____

8. How can you create new thoughts and habits that reflect God's view of beauty instead of your own?

_____

_____

9. What attributes of God do you find most beautiful? Find a passage of Scripture that illuminates each attribute. Whenever you begin to fixate on yourself— whether on your flaws or your fabulousness—replace those thoughts with ones of God's beauty, which never fades.

_____

_____

APPLICATION: CUT THE CRAP

Figure out what in your life influences you to be vain—a magazine, a TV show, a relationship, etc.—and commit to changing that habit. Stop watching, stop fixating, stop setting yourself up to fail.

God, give me the desire to stop chasing after youth and beauty and things that fail. Give me eyes to see people, including myself, the way You do. Give me strength and dignity and a sense of humor so I can laugh at my aging body, knowing this life is a blip compared to eternity with You. Help me find my worth in You and You alone. Amen.

CHAPTER 2 |||||||| Money

I know what it is to be in need, and I know what it is to have plenty. I have learned the secret of being content in any and every situation, whether well fed or hungry, whether living in plenty or in want. I can do all this through him who gives me strength.
PHILIPPIANS 4:12-13

1. What material things do you pine for? Why do you pine?

   _____

   _____

2. How has greed affected your life and your relationships, including your relationship with God?

   _____

   _____

3. Read Philippians 3:8-11. What *should* we pine for?

_____

_____

4. Read Proverbs 3:9. Do you give of your "firstfruits"?
   Why or why not?

_____

_____

5. How do you define contentment?

_____

_____

6. When do you feel most content? Most discontent?

_____

_____

7. Read Philippians 4:13. Where do your strength and security
   come from?

_____

_____

8. How would your life be different if being content was the norm?

_____

_____

9. Read Matthew 22:36-38. Since loving Jesus more combats
   our love of money, what are practical ways you can serve and
   love Jesus more every day?

_____

_____

APPLICATION: INTO THE GREEN

Look at your last couple of bank statements and credit card bills and honestly evaluate where your money goes. Ask God to show you where you're misspending and how you could honor and love him more with your finances.

God, give me a heart that is thankful for the blessings in my life, starting with You. Give me self-control and wisdom to steward my money well, and give me the ability to stand firm when temptation comes. Take away my greed and lust for stuff, and replace it with contentment and a desire for more of You. Give me a love for Jesus that keeps my eyes fixed on Him, and help me to stand firm in His strength, come what may. Amen.

CHAPTER 3 ||||||||| # Recognition

"Let not the wise boast of their wisdom
or the strong boast of their strength
or the rich boast of their riches,
but let the one who boasts boast about this:
that they have the understanding to know me,
that I am the LORD, who exercises kindness,
justice and righteousness on earth,
for in these I delight,"
declares the LORD.

JEREMIAH 9:23-24

1. What do you want to be known for?

_____

_____

2. Who do you work hard to impress?

_____

_____

3. What weaknesses do you try to hide?

_____

_____

4. Read 2 Corinthians 12:7-10. What would it look like
   for you to delight in your weaknesses instead of hiding
   them?

_____

_____

5. How has God already used your weaknesses to bring glory
   to Himself?

_____

_____

6. Read Luke 10:38-42. In what ways are you like Martha?
   Like Mary? How will you make more time to sit and listen
   to Jesus?

_____

_____

7. What does God see when He looks at you? How important
   is God's opinion of you _to you_?

_____

_____

8. Read John 3:22-36, paying close attention to the gist of verse 30. Are you content to have Jesus be the only one to get glory from your life? Why or why not?

_____

_____

9. What characteristic of God do you most want to reflect today? This month? This year?

_____

_____

APPLICATION: WANNABE

Think of a Christian woman you admire, whether from the Bible or someone you know personally—a woman known for her love of and obedience to Christ. Why specifically do you admire her? Pray that God, by His Spirit, would produce those fruits in you and that they would become more desirable to you than any worldly title.

God, give me humility, that I would allow people to see my weaknesses. Give me the desire and discipline to spend time with You each day. Give me confidence in the knowledge that You think I'm special. Help me to believe that approval from others means nothing in light of Your love for and acceptance of me, and help me to value the things You value. Help me to seek Your glory instead of my own. Amen.

CHAPTER 4 |||||||| # Relationships

*I am convinced that neither death nor life, neither angels nor
demons, neither the present nor the future, nor any powers,
neither height nor depth, nor anything else in all creation,
will be able to separate us from the love of God that is in
Christ Jesus our Lord.*

ROMANS 8:38-39

1. Who do you love more than you love God?

   _____

   _____

2. How have your relationships suffered because you haven't
   put Christ at the center of them?

   _____

   _____

3. What unfair or inappropriate expectations do you have
   of the people in your life? What steps do you need to
   take in order to change your expectations and heal your
   relationships (repenting, asking forgiveness, creating new
   habits)?

   _____

   _____

4. Why is it difficult for you to put God first?

   _____

   _____

5. Are there times when you feel closer to God? What circumstances contribute to the ebb and flow?

_____

_____

6. What are your current expectations of God?

_____

_____

7. Read Deuteronomy 4:24; 2 Samuel 22:2-4; 2 Chronicles 7:13-15; Matthew 6:25-34; 7:24-27; 11:28-30; and 1 John 3:1. What expectations does the Bible say you should have of God?

_____

_____

8. What does it take for you to faithfully spend time in God's Word?

_____

_____

9. What are some practical ways you can rely on God more and on "your people" less?

_____

_____

10. Read Matthew 22:36-40. With God in His rightful first place, what are three ways you can express His love to the people in your life today?

_____

_____

APPLICATION: LOVE TRAIN

Read one of the following passages about God's love every day this week. Meditate on it, asking God to teach you about, and open your heart to more of, His love.

Psalm 139:1-18
Psalm 56:8 (preferably in the New Living Translation)
Romans 5:6-11
Romans 8:31-39
Ephesians 1:3-14
Ephesians 3:14-19
1 John 4:9-10

God, create in me an undivided heart and right priorities. Help me to love You first, and help me to love others well. Give me wisdom to know how to spend my time so that I have enough to spend with You each day. Give me a heart that is receptive to Your love so my joy and peace and self-worth remain firmly planted in You. Amen.

CHAPTER 5 |||||||| # Parenthood

You parents—if your children ask for a loaf of bread, do you give them a stone instead? Or if they ask for a fish, do you give them a snake? Of course not! So if you sinful people know how to give good gifts to your children, how much more will your heavenly Father give good gifts to those who ask him. MATTHEW 7:9-11, NLT

1. What are your greatest strengths as a parent or as someone who influences younger generations?

   _____

   _____

2. What are your greatest fears regarding your children (or any other children, for that matter)?

   _____

   _____

3. How does your fear impact your behavior? How does your fear impact the children in your life?

   _____

   _____

4. What do you want the children you love to believe about God?

   _____

   _____

5. What do you really believe about God's goodness?

   _____

   _____

6. How does your faith in God's goodness show up in your parenting or mentoring?

   _____

   _____

7. Read Psalm 36:5; Psalm 62:8; Psalm 147:3; Mark 6:34; Acts 14:17; Romans 5:8; 2 Peter 3:9; and Revelation 4:11. What does Scripture say about God's goodness? Fill in the blank for each verse: God is good because He _____

   _____

   _____

8. Do you believe the things you just read as they relate to children? Pray that God would help you to believe—to relinquish them to His loving care.

   _____

   _____

9. What are practical ways you can trust God more with the kids in your life?

   _____

   _____

APPLICATION: PRAY IT OUT

Ask God to direct you to a verse or passage for each of your children or the children close to you. Commit to regularly praying that Scripture for them, and watch expectantly for God to work in their hearts and lives.

God, I confess that when it comes to my kids, my mommy-love eclipses my willingness to surrender to Your will and plan. Help me to trust You. Help me to rest in Your love, and help me to believe You love my children more than I do. Help me to be confident of Your goodness in all circumstances, even when my children struggle. I pray they would know You in a real way and from an early age so they would experience life at Your side. Amen.

CHAPTER 6 |||||||| # Plans ═══

The LORD is my shepherd, I lack nothing.
    He makes me lie down in green pastures,
he leads me beside quiet waters,
    he refreshes my soul.
He guides me along the right paths
    for his name's sake.

PSALM 23:1-3

1. What's your five-year plan? Describe your planning process.
   How do you make decisions?

   _____

   _____

2. Why are your plans important to you?

   _____

   _____

3. What do you think God thinks of your process? Your
   specific plans?

   _____

   _____

4. Read James 4:13-17. What plans (or part of your plan)
   have you made without consulting God first?

   _____

   _____

5. Read Jonah 1:1-3. Is God calling you to (or away from) something you've been ignoring? When was the last time you asked Him to show you what He wants your life to look like?

_____

_____

6. Read Acts 16:6-10. Tell about a time you were willing to relinquish or change your plans when God required it. And tell about a time you weren't.

_____

_____

7. Have you ever been sifted or disciplined by God, or experienced a season when you felt like an exile? How did you react? Did you draw near to God, or did you turn away from Him?

_____

_____

8. Read Psalm 23:1-3. Describe how you spend time in God's green pastures and by His quiet waters. What does that really mean in your life?

_____

_____

9. What do you think God wants you to do with your life? Scratch that—how about just this year? This week?

_____

_____

APPLICATION: LET IT GO

Write your current plans on individual pieces of paper, lay them in front of you, and then relinquish them to God in prayer. Ask for direction. Ask for clarity. Ask for resolve. If need be, do it every day, and pray that God would help you mean it.

God, I confess that You are often an afterthought when it comes to my plans. Change the way I think. Help me remember to ask You before I forge ahead, and give me discernment, wisdom, and patience as I wait on Your answers. Guide me and help me follow. Help me to mean it when I say, "Thy Kingdom come, Thy will be done." Amen.

CHAPTER 7 |||||||| # Pride

It is because of him that you are in Christ Jesus, who has become for us wisdom from God—that is, our righteousness, holiness and redemption. Therefore, as it is written: "Let the one who boasts boast in the Lord."
I CORINTHIANS 1:30-31

1. List three things you think are true about yourself.

_____

_____

2. List three things you desire to change.

_____

_____

3. Read Psalm 139:13-14; Galatians 2:20; and Hebrews 13:6. How is confidence different from pride? Where should our confidence come from?

_____

_____

4. Read John 10:27; John 14:16-17; and Romans 10:17. How do you hear from God? Are you faithful in your routine? What could you do differently or better in order to tune your ears to His voice?

_____

_____

5. Describe a time when you were appropriately humbled. Did your self-perception change? How has your life been different since?

_____

_____

6. Read John 15:5 and Hebrews 13:6. In what circumstances are you dependent on the Lord? Are there areas of your life where you're going it alone?

_____

_____

7. What are some specific ways you've experienced God's love for you?

_____

_____

8. How does God's love expose pride? How does it drive out
   pride?

   _____

   _____

9. Read Psalm 34:1-3 and Romans 14:11. A worshipful heart
   and a bended knee are the antitheses of a prideful heart.
   What is impeding your worship?

   _____

   _____

10. List your three favorite attributes of God—things so far and
    above any good in you—and praise Him for them.

    _____

    _____

APPLICATION: OUT WITH THE OLD, IN WITH THE TRUE

Read Psalm 139:23-24. Sometimes we lack self-awareness and
don't see the stuff standing between us and the Lord. Ask God to
show you anything in your heart or life that offends Him. Ask to
be sifted and changed—which is a scary request, I know. But until
we're willing to face what's already there, we'll be stunted in our
growth, stalled on the road to becoming more like Jesus.

*Dear God, I confess my pride and strong desire to do things
all by myself. I confess that pride has run amuck in my heart,
eroding my relationship with others and with You. Thank You
for being faithful to show me my sin, painful as Your work in my
life can be. Thank You for being faithful to change me, stripping*

*me of pride, self-absorption, resentment, and self-protection,
and for replacing those things with humility and the dependence
on You I so desperately need. And thank You for giving me a
worshipful heart. Lord God, You are worthy of all my praise and
deserve all the glory. Teach me to worship unencumbered by the
pride that puts me on the throne. And keep me on my knees so I
will grow and look more and more like Your Son. Amen.*

CHAPTER 8 |||||||| # Testimony

*This is the message we heard from Jesus and now declare to
you: God is light, and there is no darkness in him at all. So
we are lying if we say we have fellowship with God but go on
living in spiritual darkness; we are not practicing the truth.
But if we are living in the light, as God is in the light, then
we have fellowship with each other, and the blood of Jesus,
his Son, cleanses us from all sin.*

*If we claim we have no sin, we are only fooling ourselves
and not living in the truth. But if we confess our sins to him,
he is faithful and just to forgive us our sins and to cleanse us
from all wickedness.* I JOHN 1:5-9, NLT

1. Have you ever envied someone else's story? If so, who and
   why?

   _____

   _____

2. Describe a time God used another person to draw you closer to Him. What were the circumstances in your life at the time? How did that particular person point you to Him?

_____

_____

3. Read 2 Corinthians 2:14; Ephesians 2:4-7; and 1 John 1:5-9. What really draws people to Jesus? Do you hinder or help that goal? How?

_____

_____

4. Read Galatians 5:16-26. What does the redemptive work of the Spirit produce in us? Have you been taking credit for a particular quality He has cultivated in your heart?

_____

_____

5. What stands between you and sharing your testimony or the gospel?

_____

_____

6. Read Matthew 5:43-45 and Luke 12:51-53. Are there people in your life who have separated themselves from you because of Jesus? What should you be doing while you wait for the Lord to restore your relationship?

_____

_____

7. What do you think it means to be transparent?

_____

_____

8. In what areas of your life are you being authentic, and in what areas do you need to grow in authenticity? Be specific.

_____

_____

9. Read 1 Samuel 7:12 from the New Living Translation: "Samuel then took a large stone and placed it between the towns of Mizpah and Jeshanah. He named it Ebenezer (which means 'the stone of help'), for he said, 'Up to this point the LORD has helped us!'" Samuel wanted the people to see the rock and be reminded of what God had just done for them—it was a memorial of His work in their lives. Make a list of your Ebenezer stones.

_____

_____

10. Write your testimony, both your come-to-Jesus moment and what God is changing in you or working through you today (I was . . . , but God . . . , and now . . .).

_____

_____

APPLICATION: NEW MERCIES I SEE

Galatians 5:22-23 says, "Against such [fruit] there is no law."—in other words, there is no limit or cap on the Holy Spirit's redemptive work in our lives. What sanctifying change is God trying to make in your heart or mind right now? What spiritual fruit do you need more of? God is always at work, always writing another chapter in your life story. Pray that He would show you what He's working on, and pray that you'll surrender to it. And then get honest about it with the people in your path.

Oh, Lord, I praise You for saving me. I praise You for pulling me along the Jesus road, for picking me up when I fall, and for refusing to tolerate the sin that seeks to destroy my relationship with You. Thank You that You love me completely just as I am in this moment and that You love me too much to let me stay who I am in this moment. You are good. You are patient. You are faithful to make me more and more like Your Son, who You sent to redeem my wandering heart. Help me, God, to stay under Your pruning hand and to be honest about my struggles with myself and with the people in my life. Give me the courage and the opportunity to share the gospel and how it has changed me. Give me peace and rest in Your total acceptance and love, I pray. Amen.

CHAPTER 9 |||||||| # Obedience

This world is not our permanent home; we are looking forward to a home yet to come. Therefore, let us offer through Jesus a continual sacrifice of praise to God, proclaiming our allegiance to his name. And don't forget to do good and to share with those in need. These are the sacrifices that please God.

HEBREWS 13:14-16, NLT

1. Read Isaiah 55:8-9. Do God's plans sometimes seem unfair or unjust? Do you ever think your good or bad behavior somehow plays a part? Why or why not?

_____

_____

2. Have you ever lost someone too soon, whether to death or estrangement? In what ways did the Lord carry you? In what ways did you battle through it alone?

_____

_____

3. Read Isaiah 1:11. Do you ever obey God for the wrong reasons? What are your wrong reasons? What should the reasons be?

_____

_____

4. What sin in your life do you loathe? What sin in your life is on repeat? What do you do when the Lord convicts you?

_____

_____

5. Read 1 Peter 5:7-9. When Satan whispers in your ear, what does he say? Which of his lies do you believe?

_____

_____

6. What is grace? What does it look like in your life right now? What should it look like?

_____

_____

7. Have you experienced God by your side, closer than a brother, comforting or carrying or guiding or protecting you? When and how?

8. Read 1 Kings 19:11-12. When have you heard God's still, gentle voice? How did you respond?

_____

_____

9. Describe a time you were called to awkwardness for Jesus. Did you heed the call? What was the outcome?

_____

_____

10. Read Jeremiah 17:5-8. Are you trying to obey in your own strength, or are you asking and trusting God to give you the strength you need to obey? Confess your weakness and lack of resolve to do what's right, and ask God for help. He wants to help!

_____

_____

APPLICATION: STOP, DROP, AND PRAY

Praise God that every breath we take is rich and ripe with opportunity for obedience that pleases Him. Stop what you're doing, confess that you don't have the ability to please God on your own, and ask Him to empower you today. And ask again tomorrow and the next day and the next, lest you be led astray by Satan, who exists to twist the truth and pollute our walk with Christ.

Dear God, I praise You for grace. I praise You for being so patient when I obey for the wrong reasons, when I have a bad attitude, and when I don't extend Your grace to others. I praise You that You offer help freely, that You equip Your children for service, and that Your Word is a constant source of truth to combat Satan's lies. Help me, Lord, to live my life in a way that pleases You. I long to hear those words "Well done" from the one who saved me, is redeeming me, and is faithful to complete the work He began in my heart. Amen.

CHAPTER 10 ||||||||| # Diet Coke

The LORD is my shepherd;
   I have all that I need.
He lets me rest in green meadows;
   he leads me beside peaceful streams.
   He renews my strength.
He guides me along right paths,
   bringing honor to his name.
Even when I walk
   through the darkest valley,
I will not be afraid,
   for you are close beside me.
Your rod and your staff
   protect and comfort me.
You prepare a feast for me
   in the presence of my enemies.

You honor me by anointing my head with oil.
My cup overflows with blessings.
Surely your goodness and unfailing love will pursue me
all the days of my life,
and I will live in the house of the LORD
forever.

PSALM 23:1-6, NLT

1. Do you have a Krissie in your life—someone who inspires you with her contentment and ability to depend completely on God? What do you see in her life that you desire more of in your own?

   _____

   _____

2. What are you too dependent on? Make a list of your crutches, and explain how and when you use them.

   _____

   _____

3. How do you think the Lord views your list of coping mechanisms? Explain.

   _____

   _____

4. What are the deeper needs you're trying to meet with your crutches? Peace? Joy? Security? Take to time to pray and think through the root of your behavior.

   _____

   _____

5. Read Isaiah 30:18; Matthew 6:33; and 2 Peter 1:3-4. Make a list of the times in your life when God has provided in a way only He could.

_____

_____

6. Read Psalm 37:3-6. In what current circumstance is God teaching you dependence? Are you submitting or rebelling, and why?

_____

_____

7. Read Psalm 37:7. Describe your time with God. Is it a chore? Your main source of joy or strength? Or somewhere in between?

_____

_____

8. What steps can you take to rely on the Lord more than you currently do?

_____

_____

9. Read Matthew 4:1-11. Why do you think Jesus fasted? What implications does His fasting have for you?

_____

_____

10. Write out Matthew 22:37-38. Describe how loving God with your heart, soul, and mind should impact the way you spend your day. Are you loving God with all you are? Why or why not?

_____

_____

APPLICATION: ROCK-AND-ROLL WISDOM

Read through your list of crutches from question 2 as Mick Jagger's "(I Can't Get No) Satisfaction" plays in your head. Compare what you're settling for to Psalm 23. Crazy, right? Use your prayer time this week to ask God for wisdom and self-control to bring your needs and your *likes* into a proper balance that will glorify God and satisfy your deepest longings.

Dear God, thank You that no stronghold in my life is too strong for You to change. Thank You that in spite of my constant settling for things that offer fleeting satisfaction, You remain faithful, and Your love for me doesn't change. Please change me. Please show me where I'm inappropriately relying on things or people instead of You. I confess my desire to be instantly gratified and my tendency to wander from You and Your promise to truly satisfy. Change me, Lord. Change my instincts. Change what I love. Give me a desire—a thirst—for You and Your unique and total sufficiency, and give me the discipline and the wisdom to make life-giving choices each day. Amen.

CHAPTER 11 ||||||||| # Happiness

*I once thought these things were valuable, but now I
consider them worthless because of what Christ has done.
Yes, everything else is worthless when compared with the
infinite value of knowing Christ Jesus my Lord. For his sake
I have discarded everything else, counting it all as garbage,
so that I could gain Christ and become one with him. I no
longer count on my own righteousness through obeying the
law; rather, I become righteous through faith in Christ.
For God's way of making us right with himself depends on
faith. I want to know Christ and experience the mighty
power that raised him from the dead. I want to suffer with
him, sharing in his death, so that one way or another I will
experience the resurrection from the dead!*
PHILIPPIANS 3:7-11, NLT

1. What are the things you want most out of life?

   _____

   _____

2. When has your life seemed the most out of control?

   _____

   _____

3. How do you typically respond to the twists and turns,
   disappointments, and imperfections of life?

   _____

   _____

4. Read Matthew 7:24-27. Where does your hope come from? In other words, where have you built your proverbial house?

_____

_____

5. Read Psalm 25:4-6. What does it mean to hope in God?

_____

_____

6. How has your view of God changed as you've gotten older and experienced more of life and of Him?

_____

_____

7. Read Philippians 3:10-11. What does it mean to "suffer with Christ"? Are you willing to suffer, as Paul was?

_____

_____

8. How would your life be different if you "looked up"? If your hope was rooted in spending eternity with God in the new Eden?

_____

_____

9. Read Proverbs 8:17; Isaiah 40:29; 42:6; 54:10; John 14:27; 16:22; Romans 8:28; 1 Corinthians 2:9; 10:13; and Philippians 4:19. What are some of God's promises we can cling to while we wait for eternity to commence? (Notice that the book of Isaiah rules.)

_____

_____

10. Read Colossians 3:1-4. Is Christ your life?

_____

_____

APPLICATION: HOMEWARD BOUND

Write down the changes you want to make in your life to reflect that God's Word is true, His promises are real, and our home is in heaven.

God, change my life by giving me an eternal perspective. Help me hope for what I don't yet see. Help me remember that nothing here will ever be perfect but that You are, and someday the perfection You intended will be restored. Make me patient, and grant me joy in the waiting. Lead me so that my life will mean something in light of Your eternal Kingdom. You are worthy of my allegiance, worthy of my hope, and worthy of my praise. Be Lord of my life, today and every day. Amen.

CHAPTER 12 |||||||||| # Freedom

I don't mean to say that I have already achieved these things or that I have already reached perfection. But I press on to possess that perfection for which Christ Jesus first possessed me. No, dear brothers and sisters, I have not achieved it, but I focus on this one thing: Forgetting the past and looking forward to what lies ahead, I press on to reach the end of the race and receive the heavenly prize for which God, through Christ Jesus, is calling us. PHILIPPIANS 3:12-14, NLT

1. Read John 8:31-32. What do you think it means to be free in Jesus?

_____

_____

2. What influences the way you see your spiritual freedom? Your upbringing (whether you've accepted how you were raised or you're rebelling against it)? Pop culture? Scripture? Justification of sin?

_____

_____

3. What do you want to be free *from*? Addiction? Selfishness? Fear? Pride? List everything you can think of.

_____

_____

4. Read Romans 6:22 and Galatians 5:1. In what ways are you still acting like a slave to your sin? Is there something in your life you're reticent to let go of completely?

_____

_____

5. Read Colossians 1:21-23. What do you want to do with your God-given freedom? Be your own master? Or glorify the one who freed you in the first place? Maybe a mixture of both? Explain and be honest.

_____

_____

6. Read Ephesians 3:12 and 1 Peter 2:16. What does it mean to live as God's slave?

_____

_____

7. Read Galatians 5:22-23. By the power of the Holy Spirit, we are free to exhibit the fruit of the Spirit—"against such things there is no law." In other words, there's no limit to God's goodness expressed in our lives. Which of these fruits do you need more of? Ask God for it.

_____

_____

8. Read Ephesians 6:10-17. What piece of spiritual armor are you forgetting to wear? How is Satan exploiting your vulnerability as a result?

_____

_____

9. God usually convicts us of one or two "biggies" at a time—
   or in my case, one chapter at a time. Prayerfully identify
   your biggest area of struggle—the one God wants to change
   in you right now. What piece of God's armor specifically
   applies to the stronghold He wants to bring down, and what
   will you do to suit up?

   _____

   _____

10. Read Philippians 3:12-14. Is our desire for perfection part of
    our wiring? If so, how was it intended to be fulfilled?

    _____

    _____

APPLICATION: BRIDGET JONES IT

In the hope of starting a new chapter in your life, make your
own list of stats that reflects your relationship with Jesus right
now. Then make your resolutions about how to get to your new
chapter. (You can use the example below or go rogue and make
up your own.)

Spiritual Status:

Strangleholds:

Hopes:

Resolve to . . .

*Dear God, thank You that in You there is freedom. Help me to see
it more clearly. Help me to desire You and the life You offer—to*

value the things You value, like kindness, gentleness, patience, and self-control. Change the way I see the world and all the things that masquerade as freedom giving when in reality they enslave. Thank You that You have conquered sin and death, and that You offer us life in Christ. Make me more like Him. Help me desire to be more like Him. Help me love You with my whole being. Lift my eyes to heaven, where my longing for perfection will be fulfilled. Amen.